THE WORLD'S GREAT STORIES

THE WORLD'S GREAT STORIES

Fifty-Five Legends That Live Forever

Retold by

LOUIS UNTERMEYER

Illustrated by
MAE GERHARD

M. Evans and Company, Inc., *New York*

Except for that part of "Androcles and the Lion," which was published in *Legendary Animals* (Golden Press, 1963) and part of "The Mouse Tower on the Rhine" from *Blue Rhine, Black Forest* (Harcourt, Brace and Company, 1930, 1958), all the versions of the stories in this book appear in print for the first time.

The book itself could not have been completed—could not even have begun—had I not relied on the constant aid of Homer, Livy, Plutarch, Malory, Pauline Rush Evans, who suggested it, and Ethel Connor, who typed it.

L.U.

Library of Congress Catalog Card No. 64-23030
ISBN 0-87131-496-7 (Paperbound)

Copyright © 1964 by Louis Untermeyer
Illustrations © 1964 by M. Evans and Company, Inc.

M. Evans and Company, Inc.
216 East 49 Street
New York, New York 10017

Design by Edward Gorey

Manufactured in the United States of America

9 8 7 6 5 4 3 2 1

CONTENTS

Before You Read This Book

HE STORIES in this book are not to be read merely as fantasies. Though more than a few are touched with magic, they are not fairy tales. Most legends have their origins in history, in events as they actually occurred or were thought to have occurred. These stories have survived, not because they are based on fact, but because they touch on fundamental traits of human nature.

We hear echoes of such tales and legends not only in our literature but also in our language: in such phrases as "rich as Croesus," "crossing the Rubicon," "these are my jewels," "cutting the Gordian knot." Even such single words as "Eureka!" "colossal," "mausoleum," and "labyrinth" are reminders of their ancient sources.

Some of these stories are related to fables that express general or moral truths, others are frankly amazing and frequently amusing. But all have the quality of permanence; they have outlasted history for they are rich in characters that have the power to stir the imagination. They have the deathless spirit of tales which have been told countless times and will be retold as long as there are listeners.

In this narration I have imagined certain incidents, supplied fresh details and added dialogue. The bases of these stories, however, are unaltered, full of the power which continues to keep them vividly alive and forever new.

L. U.

9

THESEUS AND THE LABYRINTH

... *The Struggle with the Minotaur*

THESEUS was the son of King Aegeus, but his father had gone to another kingdom while he was still a baby. Before leaving, Aegeus had put a sword and a pair of sandals under a large stone and said to the mother of Theseus:

"When our son is strong enough to roll away that stone, let him take the sword and sandals and bring them to me."

As a child Theseus was strong and fearless. His toys were bows and arrows; he made friends not only with fawns but with wild stags, and played with savage boars as though they were household pets. His mother was proud of his daring and encouraged him to greater and greater feats of strength. Watching him grow up, she took joy in his prowess with spears and javelins. She teased him into picking up stones, small stones for her garden at first, then gradually larger and larger rocks. There was only one difficulty: Theseus saddened her by continually asking about his father.

"The time will come when I can tell you all you need to know," she would say. "When you are a little older—and a little stronger—when you can drive a chariot, bend the stoutest bow, throw the largest spear, and move the heaviest stone. Then you will learn about your father."

Theseus was impatient for the promised time. He set his mind to becoming the strongest youth in the land. As he grew out of boyhood he kept increasing his strength by taming wild horses, hunting bears, fighting wild bulls, wrestling with champions, doing everything possible to harden each muscle in his pliant body. At eighteen his mother felt he was ready. She led him to a secret place next to a temple and pointed to the stone that Aegeus had placed there.

"If you can lift that," she said, "you will not have to ask me who your father is or where he is."

Theseus bent down and slipped his fingers under one edge of the stone. It did not stir. Then, straining every muscle, he felt it budge; it gave an inch. Tugging until his sinews cracked, he lifted it up to his knees and, with a shout, rolled it over. In the hole underneath, he spied something wrapped in purple linen.

"Your father left it there for you," said his mother. "Now you will know where to find him."

Theseus unwrapped the folds and saw a pair of golden sandals and a sword of bronze, its gold handle set with crystals and precious gems. It was a royal sword. The blade was engraved with a design of crowns and palaces and, near the hilt, Theseus read this line:

This blade belongs to Aegeus, King of Athens.

"Now I know," said Theseus. "I will wait no longer to find my father."

"Yes," said his mother, "I must let you go. Your father has need of you. Word has come to me that your father is in trouble. He is no longer master in his own house. A sorceress rules him, and his brother's sons conspire openly against him. You are his heir, you should be at his side. But Athens is far from here. The ways are treacherous, with giants in the mountains and robbers in the passes. Take a troop of men with you for protection so that I won't have to fear for you."

"No," replied Theseus. "If I am meant to make this journey, I am meant to make it by myself. Nothing can keep a man from his destiny. If I am to prove myself my father's son, I must go alone."

Next morning, with the sword fastened to his girdle and the sandals in a sack, Theseus set out for Athens. His way led through narrow glens, rocky ledges, and paths so overgrown and entangled that he had to retrace his steps more than once. Toward dusk he found the path again; a flickering fire in the distance seemed to promise a welcome. However, when he approached the fire his way was blocked. A monstrous thick-set giant of a man stood in his way.

"This is my road," he said. "No one passes without tribute."

"All roads are free," said Theseus quietly. "I do not stop to make payments on the open road."

"You will stop," said the man, "and this will stop you." He held up a massive iron club. "My father, Hephaestus, the god of fire, gave it to me. He forged it in the flames of the underworld and told me I would never need any other weapon. That's why I am called Corynetes, the Club-Bearer, and that's why, if you want to pass, you will give me that pretty sword and whatever you are carrying in that handsome sack."

"I give nothing for nothing," said Theseus. "Take them if you can."

The Club-Bearer swung his deadly weapon, but Theseus sprang nimbly to one side and drew his sword. Leaping within the circle of the swinging club, he struck at the giant. It was scarcely a struggle. Before the Club-Bearer could recover his balance, Theseus plunged his father's sword upwards through the giant's throat. The hardest task was to roll the huge body to one side. Then he slept beside the fire. In the morning he resumed his journey.

His next adventure was with Sinis, the Pine-Bender. Sinis was a killer as well as a robber. He watched for travelers, then snared, bound, and stripped them of everything. After he had plundered his victims, Sinis would bind them hand and foot, pull down two pine trees, tie his prey to the tops, then let the trees spring apart and tear them to pieces.

Theseus had been warned about Sinis. When he entered the dark pine wood and heard a rope whistling above his head, he quickly caught the loop. Before the killer could recover from his surprise, Theseus threw the loop around the Pine-Bender's neck. Then he pulled down two pines and bound the killer to the tops.

"It is your turn," he said. "Now, Pine-Bender, bend your pines."

The next threat encountered was Sciron. He was known as Sciron the Kicker because, for permission to pass along the cliff road he occupied, he would force travelers to wash his feet. While they were doing so, he kicked them off the cliff to the gulf below where lived a huge tortoise who, unlike other turtles, fed upon human flesh.

"Do you know the price if you wish to proceed further?" asked Sciron, stretching out his legs. "Unless you wash my feet here I will have to dispose of you elsewhere. My tortoise is hungry today."

"I bend my knee to no man," said Theseus.

"And who are you to speak so insolently?" sneered Sciron.

"I am Prince Theseus, son of King Aegeus, and I will wait here no longer."

"It will be a pleasure, a new experience, to have my feet washed by a prince. Perhaps this club will persuade you."

Before Sciron could bring the weight of his spiked club down on Theseus' head, Theseus lunged at him and, with his great strength,

pinned the would-be killer against the side of the cliff. Forcing him
to his knees, Theseus took away Sciron's club and threw it into the
gulf.

"Would you care to follow your club now, or would you rather
wash my feet first?" he said.

Sullenly Sciron rose and stooped to the task. Theseus did not let
him finish. Instead he gave Sciron so mighty a kick that it hurled
him over the edge of the cliff. "There," he cried, "join the unfor-
tunates you have thrown there. Now you can feed the tortoise yourself."

Theseus resumed his journey light of heart and full of the joy of
the road. Nearing Athens, he passed into Eleusis, where he was
threatened by its cruel ruler. Theseus wrestled with him and broke
his neck. The natives were grateful for being rid of this tyrant and
wanted to make Theseus their king. But he told them he was on a
solemn quest, that he must go on to Athens.

"Alas, my lord," said one of the men of Eleusis, "you will never
get there. Athens is not far, but it can be reached only after you
have overcome the most terrible obstacle."

"And what, or who, might that be?" asked Theseus.

"Procrustes," the man answered. "He is not a giant or a monster
or any evil-looking creature. On the contrary, he is a soft-spoken
person who will greet you with the greatest courtesy. He will show
you his fine home, invite you to partake of his hospitality, entertain
you with the choicest foods, and offer you the softest bed."

"It sounds alluring," said Theseus. "What have I to fear?"

"The bed. He will tell you it is a bed like no other in the world,
that it fits everyone who sleeps in it no matter what his size. And
he is right, the bed is unique. There is a mechanical saw hidden at
one end and a secret rope-machine at the other. When his guest is
asleep, iron arms come down from the ceiling and hold him so that
he cannot move. If the sleeper is too short for the bed, the rope-
machine stretches him until his bones are pulled out of their joints.
If he is too long, the saw just lops off his limbs. Oh yes, the bed fits
every comer, no matter how short or tall he may be."

"Thank you for your warning," said Theseus. "I look forward to
meeting this charming host."

Then he went on. Two days later, as Theseus began the ascent of
Mount Parnes, he was accosted by a person of noble bearing.
Dressed in purple garments embroidered in gold, he wore a heavy

gold collar around his neck and bracelets sparkling with jewels on his wrists.

"You are welcome to my domain," said the man. "You are a stranger, and strangers are particularly welcome, for they are favored by the gods. I can see that you have come a long way, and it is now almost night. My home here will provide rest. You will, I promise, dine well. And I can assure you of a sound sleep."

Theseus looked at the hypocrite with a crooked smile. "I am sure of that," he said, and went into the house.

The dinner was everything that had been promised. There was rare venison and rich pastry and a heady red wine. At the end of the meal Procrustes accompanied Theseus up the stairs.

"You must be tired, and I shall not keep you from the rest you need," he said. "Let me show you my magic bed—I call it a magic bed because it is made to fit whoever sleeps in it."

"It looks like an unusual bed indeed. It seems to have a peculiar structure," said Theseus. "How is one supposed to lie in it?"

"It's quite simple," said Procrustes. "You just relax and stretch out like this." And he lay down for a moment.

The moment was enough. Theseus leaped upon him and, whipping out a rope he had hidden, tied Procrustes to the bed.

"You seem to be a little too long," said Theseus. "We must remedy that." And he performed what was necessary. "Now," he added, after he had done what Procrustes had done so often to others, "now you fit perfectly." Then he went his way.

There were no further incidents on the road. When Theseus entered the king's palace in Athens he saw his father's nephews idling about the courtyard. They were playing games, gambling, and drinking. One of them looked up. "What do you want?" he said. "Be brief. You see we are busy."

"I have come to see your master," said Theseus.

They laughed rudely. "We are all masters here," said the one who had spoken. "You should see the mistress if you are looking for lodging; she runs the house.

Theseus brushed by them and went into the great hall. King Aegeus was sitting with Medea, the sorceress. She knew who Theseus was, although his father did not recognize him. Her magic arts told her that if father and son were reunited she would lose her power over Aegeus. So she dissembled and smiled.

"We should honor the young stranger," she said in a honey-sweet voice. "While you converse I shall prepare a welcome worthy of a hero."

Some instinct had warned Theseus not to reveal himself. He said nothing while Aegeus sat wondering and Medea, taking a flask from her bosom, filled a goblet and offered it to him.

"It is a gracious gesture," said Theseus, "as gracious as the lady who offers it. But I would profane the cup by taking the first draft. Will you not drink first?"

Medea trembled. "I——dare not. Wine makes me ill."

Theseus' face grew stern. "You will pledge the king with this cup," he said, and pressed it against her lips. Medea thrust the cup away; it fell to the ground. The wine hissed on the pavement and the marble dissolved as a cloud of evil-smelling smoke drifted through the hall. The sorceress shrieked an incantation, and out of the smoke there sprang a dragon attached to a chariot. Medea leaped into the magic car and flew away.

Theseus turned to his father.

"I have cleared the roads of robbers, murderers, and other monsters," he said. "I have rid your house of witchcraft and poison. My good fortune has been wonderful. But there is a greater wonder." And he showed Aegeus the sword and the sandals.

Aegeus threw his arms around the hero's neck and wept. "My son, my son!" he kept repeating. "My son!" Then, as he grew quieter, he said, "I should be overjoyed that you have come at last, but my joy is tempered with sadness, for you come at an unhappy time."

"Perhaps I was fated to come at this time to help you," said Theseus. "What causes your unhappiness?"

"There is a curse upon me," answered Aegeus. "It is a strong curse. It dates from the time when young men came to Athens from all over to take part in the festival games of racing, wrestling, boxing, weight-hurling, and spear-throwing. The son of King Minos of Crete was one of the contestants, and he died here. His death was a mystery. Some said he was killed by the spear of a jealous rival; some said it was an accident. Minos sailed here from the island of Crete with an army. We were too ill-equipped and too ashamed to give battle. Wearing deep mourning, the elders and I went to Minos asking forgiveness for what had happened. 'You shall have mercy,' said Minos, 'on one condition. Every seven years I will send a ship to collect a tribute, and every seven years you will send me seven of your strongest youths and seven of your loveliest maidens.' There

was nothing to do but agree. I have kept my promise. Now it is the seventh year, time for the sacrifice, and the ship from Crete is approaching."

"We could defy Minos by burning his ship," said Theseus. "I'm not a party to this promise, so I could do it."

"I admire your reckless courage," said Aegeus. "But what would be the result? Minos would send a mighty fleet crammed with his soldiers. He has many powerful allies, and we small independent states are too weak to resist him. The promise must be kept."

"Then let me go with the seven youths and seven maidens. Why should I, your son, stay here idle, like your worthless nephews? I have freed the world of many vicious creatures. Why can I not go to Crete and kill Minos?"

"Because the youths and maidens never return; they are doomed. You would be only one more sacrifice. I have not told you all. Minos had Daedalus, the master-craftsman, build a special prison for his captives. It is not like any other prison, for it is cut into solid rock and so designed, so cunningly constructed with winding and intertwining passages that, once inside, no one can find a way out. In his maze, which he calls the Labyrinth, there lurks an incredible killer, a hideous thing known as the Minotaur. It has the body of a man, but its head is that of a ferocious bull with the teeth of a lion. It is to this devouring monster that the youths and maidens are sacrificed."

"Let me go," pleaded Theseus. "My sword has brought me through worse dangers. It will sever the head of this Minotaur."

"Alas, my son, it cannot," said Aegeus. "By Minos' orders, all weapons and armor are removed before the victim is thrown into the Labyrinth. Yet this king has an evil sense of humor: he has pledged that if anyone could slay the monster with his bare hands, then there would be no further need of tribute."

"The more you speak, the more determined I am to go. My hands have never failed me. I promise you we will all return."

"Go then, and my prayers go with you," said Aegeus. "It is a ship of death on which you will embark. Its hull is black and its sails are black. When you return—if you return—take down the black sails and hoist white sails in their place. Then, as I scan the sea, I shall know that the ship carries good tidings."

Ten days later the black-sailed ship landed in Crete and the youths and maidens were brought to the palace at Knossos, the royal city Daedalus had built for King Minos. They stood before the

king clad in mourning—all except Theseus who had dressed himself
in bright colors.

"And who are you so improperly clothed for sacrifices?" inquired
Minos. "Who has the impudence to garb himself gaily as if for a
day of rejoicing?"

"I am the son of Aegeus whom you have wronged," replied
Theseus. "And I have not come to be sacrificed. I have come to free
the people of Athens from an unjust promise."

"Brave words," said Minos with a cold smile. "I presume you
know how to carry them out. All you have to do is to dispose of the
Minotaur with your bare hands."

"That is what I intend to do," said Theseus calmly. "I ask only
one favor. Let me be the first to face the monster."

"The favor is granted. You will face him in the morning. I do
not expect to see you after that."

That night King Minos' daughter, Ariadne, knocked softly at
Theseus' door. She had fallen in love with the youth as he stood, so
proud and unafraid and defiant, in front of her father.

"You are too young, too brave, to die," she said. "I have drugged
the guards' wine, and you can escape now. Hurry, go at once to the
shore. There is a ship waiting, and no one will know until you have
sailed."

"I thank you, lady," said Theseus. "You are as kind as you are
noble. But I cannot go. There is something that must be done, and
I must do it. Too many youths and maidens have been sacrificed to
the vengeance of the king and the hungry lust of the Minotaur."

"But even if you slay the Minotaur—and you may be the one man
strong enough to do it—what then? How will you find your way
out of the Labyrinth? Do you think you can do this, too? I know
better. You will only lose yourself in hundreds of dark twists and
turnings. You will die there. But see, I have brought something to
help you."

Theseus looked and saw it was a pine cone, a strange sort of gift.
Then he noticed that around it was wound yards of stout string,
the way thread is wound around a spool. He understood the meaning of the token and, kneeling, he kissed Ariadne's small hands and
little feet. Sad with love and longing, she left him.

In the morning Theseus was taken to the Labyrinth. As soon as
the guards left him, he fastened one end of Ariadne's string to a
jutting stone and, carrying the cone carefully around corners so as
not to break the thread, he went on. For a while he walked down
a passage that was feebly lit; then the last trace of light disappeared

and he was in total darkness. He felt his way among wet walls, slimy rocks, and slippery caverns. At last he came to a place that was large and flat. A faint light filtered through a hole in the rock-roof. He looked down, saw the ground littered with bones, and knew that this was where he should wait.

He did not have to wait long. First he heard a rustling of earth, then a thudding, then a sniffing, then a deep rumble, then a loud roar. The Minotaur had discovered where he was.

For a moment the monster eyed Theseus silently. Soon it began to move its slavering jaws and, pawing the ground, made ready to trample its victim. Then it rushed straight at him. Theseus was prepared. He had scooped up a handful of loose earth and, stepping nimbly aside, he threw it right into the monster's eyes. Momentarily blinded, the Minotaur bellowed and tossed its head wildly. Before it could recover from its confusion, Theseus had his hands on its throat. The monster threshed about but could not free itself. They wrestled, fell, rolled over on one another. Theseus never loosened his grip. At last he pinned the Minotaur's head to the ground and pushed its nose into the earth. He held it there until there was no breath left in the brute's body. Then, with Ariadne's thread, he found his way back into the sunlight.

"Aegeus kept his promise," said Minos, when Theseus stood before him with the youths and maidens. "I will keep mine. I don't know by what means or by what miracle you accomplished what you did, but you did it. Therefore you and the others are free. The ship is ready for you. Farewell." And Ariadne echoed tearfully, "Fare well."

Theseus signalled to Ariadne with his eyes. She understood and, as soon as he and the others were on board, Ariadne slipped into the ship to join her beloved.

Only one thing marred the homecoming. In his joy and haste to return Theseus had forgotten to change the sails. When Aegeus, watching from a high rock, saw the ship coming in with black sails, his heart broke. He fell from the rock into the sea which, ever afterward, has been called the Aegean Sea.

Mourning was mixed with rejoicing as the youths and maidens were reunited with their families. The Athenians cheered as the wreath of victory was presented to Theseus. He waved it aside. Nor was he gladdened when they brought the crown and proclaimed him king. He had come a long and hazardous way to find his father and, at the height of his triumph, he had lost him.

DAEDALUS AND ICARUS

...The First Men to Fly

EN have always been dreamers, and perhaps their oldest dream has been a dream of flying. Watching birds spread their wings and soar into space, people of the past must have longed for the day when they would be no longer earthbound and could, somehow, find a way to lift themselves skyward and sail through the air.

The Athenian, Daedalus, was one of those dreamers. But, besides being a dreamer, he was also a doer. It was Daedalus, whose very name meant "the cunning worker," who designed some of the most fabulous gardens of his day; who was the architect of the most magnificent palaces in Crete; who, as a sculptor, was so superb a craftsman that his statues seemed to breathe——it was rumored that they could speak to their creator. And it was Daedalus who had planned the amazing Labyrinth for King Minos.

After the Labyrinth had been completed, King Minos feared that Daedalus might build another Labyrinth or an even more secret structure for someone else. So he had him shut up in a high stone tower. Daedalus with the help of his young son, Icarus, managed to escape from that stronghold. But he was still a prisoner on the island of Crete. There was no land in sight to which he could swim; every boat that left the island was searched. It was then that Daedalus returned to his old dream: the dream of flying.

"There is no way of winning our freedom by land or by sea," he told Icarus. "But," he added, as he watched the sea-gulls hover and rise, "there is the air."

That same day he put his dream to work. "Before we can fly, we must have wings," he said. "And before we have wings, we must have feathers. Let us begin by gathering feathers of every sort, every feather we can find."

Days were spent picking up feathers along the shore, trapping gulls to get their long pinions, assorting their finds. Meanwhile, Daedalus watched the way the birds took off; he studied their manner of rising and how they sustained their flight. He examined the wing structure of some of the captured birds and learned the adjustment of the smallest bones and the placement of the lightest feather.

Then he began to build a wing. With thin flexible pieces of wood he made a frame, delicate but strong. To this he fastened various sized feathers with thread and wax. He pressed the small feathers toward the inside of the skeleton wing, arranged the larger feathers in rows at the outside, and gave the whole a curvature like the wings of a huge bird.

At last Daedalus had a pair of wings greater than those of the largest bird. He fastened them to his shoulder, spread his arms, and lifted himself above the ground. The first attempt was clumsy. He wavered, lost his balance and, fluttering desperately, he fell. But he had done what no man before him had ever accomplished. He had left the earth, if only for a few minutes. He had flown!

His second flight was different. He learned now how to control the motions, how to take advantage of the air-currents and float, how to glide smoothly instead of frantically. After his third flight, he could dip and soar and hang poised as securely as any gull. Then Daedalus made a pair of smaller wings for Icarus, taught him the flying motions, and, after a while, let him practice in ever-widening circles. He warned the boy about being too eager.

It was weeks before the time came when Daedalus felt it was safe to risk an escape from the island. He had planned it carefully: they were to fly across the water to Sicily. Before they took off, Daedalus cautioned Icarus again.

"Remember, my son, to keep to the right altitude," he told him. "Do not fly too low, for if you do, the spray from the sea will clog the wings and make them too heavy. On the other hand, if you fly too high, the heat of the sun will melt the wax that holds the feathers together." With these words, father and son rose into the air.

They flew easily, side by side, steadily, serenely. People ran out of their houses to gaze at the unbelievable sight; farmers lifted their hands from the plow to shield their eyes; shepherds forgot

about their sheep. As the pair glided over the sea, sailors let go of their ropes and their oars to stare and wonder.

For the two flyers it was a continual excitement—much too exciting for Icarus. Unlike Daedalus, who controlled himself with every stroke of his wings, Icarus became reckless with this new sense of power. He beat his wings ever more rapidly, rose higher, skimmed through low-hanging clouds, and thrashed toward the heavens.

"Come back!" shouted Daedalus. "Down! Come down! Remember ——the sun!"

But Icarus, giddy with youth and the sheer joy of freedom, laughed and continued to soar upwards. Soon he was beyond the reach of his father's voice. He looked down, exulting in the height. The island of Crete seemed no larger than a small boat bobbing in a pond; ships looked like toys scattered on a blue floor. He loved the feel of sun on his shoulders; he shouted with joy.

Daedalus could barely hear him. Then the shout grew louder, closer, and Daedalus knew it was not a shout of joy but a cry of terror. The blazing sun had done its cruel work. The wax had melted, feathers were dropping from the wings, and Icarus was falling. There was no way to save him. Down he came, hurtling through the air, a helpless bird whose wings had been broken. Daedalus flew down after him, but it was too late. Icarus had sunk into the sea. A few feathers rose and fell on the waves.

When the body of Icarus floated to the surface, Daedalus, heavily burdened, flew with it to land. There he buried his son along the shore of the sea that, ever since, had been called the Icarian Sea.

Then, weeping, he took off his wings. He never flew again.

THE WOODEN HORSE

...How Troy Fell

 HE fighting before the gates of Troy had been going on for almost ten years. There were fierce individual contests between Greeks and Trojans, as well as countless larger clashes during the long siege of the city by the Greeks. Many valiant heroes had been slain: the noble Paris and Hector on the Trojan side, Patroclus and Achilles among the Greek warriors. The struggle had been watched most anxiously by the beleaguered Trojans, especially by King Priam, Queen Hecuba, and their daughter Cassandra, a prophetess who foresaw the tragic end for Troy. It was watched by Helen of Sparta too, Helen whose beauty had caused young Paris to steal her from her husband, King Menelaus, and thus brought on the war.

The Trojans had successfully resisted and they continued to hold off their adversaries. Their high-walled town was invulnerable. Secure behind battlements which the Greeks could not scale, the men of Troy hurled rocks, spears, and arrows with devastating effect through hidden loopholes.

Toward the end of the ninth year the Greeks decided to make one more mass assault. Again they were thrown back and forced to retreat to their ships lying in the harbor. There they held a painful council. Some were for new methods of attack; some for an attempt to tunnel under the walls; others wanted to abandon the siege and the idea of ever subduing Troy. There was much head-shaking followed by a sullen silence. Then a tall figure came forward. It was Calchas, the soothsayer, a man who seldom spoke.

"I had a vision last night," he said. "I saw a hawk in pursuit of a dove. The hawk was, of course, much faster and was about to plummet down upon its victim when the dove flew into a hole in a

cliff. The keen-eyed hawk saw where the dove had gone, but there was no way for such a large bird to get its talons inside the hiding place. So it flew away. But it flew only a short distance, then concealed itself behind a thick bush. After a while the dove ventured out, looked around, and took to the air. A moment later it was struck down by the hawk."

"It is a fitting parable," said Odysseus, the shrewdest of the Greeks. "We should not give up our pursuit, but we must pretend to admit defeat."

"I don't understand," objected the slow-witted Menelaus. "After all we have gone through, to pretend to be defeated is ignoble. Pretense is cowardly."

"Calchas is a prophet as well as a teller of parables," said Odysseus, patiently. "What he suggests is a wise thing. At the moment the dove of Troy sits securely in its hole. We are the outwitted hawk. Therefore, we will set fire to the camp and take to our ships. Like the hawk we will fly away. But we will not fly far. We will anchor the ships a few miles away and lie unseen behind the island of Tenedos. There we will wait for a signal."

"But how will we know when the dove is ready to leave its safe place?" asked Menelaus. "And who is to give the signal?"

"That will all be taken care of," said Odysseus. "If we cannot triumph by force, then we must conquer by cunning. What we must do is trick the Trojans to their doom. We must become woodsmen and carpenters, cut down the trees growing on the mountain beyond the town and hew the trunks into planks."

"And then?" said the puzzled Menelaus.

"Then," answered Odysseus. "We will build a horse. An immense wooden horse, huge and hollow. It will hold you and me and a dozen or so of our best men, fully armed. The rest will board the ships and sail as though for home. We will leave just one man in the camp. We will leave Sinon, who will play the role of a deserter, a traitor. He will stay behind to be discovered by the Trojans. When he is seized, perhaps beaten, he will surely be questioned by them. They will be told what I shall tell him to say. Then we shall act."

In three days the wooden horse was completed. On the midnight of the third day, the camp was set on fire, the ships set sail, and picked men, wrapping their armor in soft cloths to deaden any suspicious sound, climbed into the horse.

The next morning the Trojans looked with unbelieving eyes at what had been the camp of the enemy. It was empty. Black smoke arose from smoldering tents; the ships that had been drawn on the beach for so long a time were gone. The ground was bare; not a soldier was in sight.

Amazed, the Trojans stood motionless for a while. Then, in a sudden wave of rejoicing, they ran through the opened gates. They found nothing but fragments and ruins, discarded pots, pans, and other utensils, broken spears, discarded shields, odds and ends that seemed to have been abandoned in haste. They were still rummaging cautiously about the charred remainders when, in a clearing untouched by the flames, they noticed the wooden horse.

"What does it mean?" said one of the Trojans. "Where did it come from? And what is it doing here?"

"Perhaps it is the Greeks' idol," said another, "left behind because they were in a hurry."

"Perhaps," said a third, "they left it as a symbol, a token of peace."

"Whatever it is, beware of it!" said a warning voice. It was the voice of the priest Laocoön. "Beware of gifts from the Greeks! Do ten years of fighting against treacherous invaders mean nothing to you? I tell you this is another of their tricks. I say, whatever it is, do not touch it!"

Since they not only respected Laocoön but feared his powers of prophecy, the Trojans drew back. As they hesitated, the sea-god Poseidon, who was on the side of the Greeks, sent two enormous sea-serpents from the ocean's depths. Swiftly they rose from the waters and swept across the shore until they reached the crowd. Before a spear could be thrown or a sword lifted, the frightful creatures wrapped their scaly coils around Laocoön and his two sons and crushed them to death.

The Trojans were transfixed with consternation and horror. Then one of them spoke up.

"It is a sign, a good omen—at least for us. Laocoön was punished for speaking against the wooden horse, which surely is sacred. It must be a gift from the gods."

Again there was indecision. Some wanted to set up the wooden horse as an object of worship; others were for putting fire to it. While they were arguing, a shout was heard, and a group of Trojans came from a corner of the camp dragging with them a miserable looking Greek. They threw him down before King Priam.

"Don't kill me," he cried. "You hate me for being a Greek, but you can't hate the Greeks as much as I do."

"Why do you hate the Greeks?" asked Priam. "And why are you here?"

"I was their prisoner, O king," answered Sinon, as instructed by Odysseus. "Because I got into an angry dispute with the prophet Calchas, they were going to offer me as a sacrifice. But there wasn't time for it, and when they departed I was purposely left behind. They hoped you would kill me as soon as you found me, before I told the truth."

"And what is the truth?" said Priam.

"While I was in prison I heard the guards discussing something about a wooden horse. It was built, they said, as an offering to Athena, the goddess who is Odysseus' special protectress. It is an all-powerful figure and will protect anyone who possesses it. A city that enshrines it will be impregnable."

"Why then," continued Priam, "did they leave it here?"

"For one thing," said Sinon smoothly, "because it was much too large to take with them. For another thing or, rather, for the same reason, they made it so large and heavy that no matter what happened, it could never be taken into your city."

This was all the crowd needed. They accepted the challenge. Putting rollers under the horse's feet and ropes around its neck, they pulled, pushed, and tugged the huge horse into the very center of Troy. There they placed wreaths about it, and offered prayers of thanks for their deliverance. The war was over! The war was over, and the victory was theirs! They sang and danced all day, making up for the bitter years of privation by carousing all night. They wore themselves out with joy.

In the darkest hour before dawn, when all Troy slumbered, Sinon opened the concealed door of the wooden horse, and out crept Odysseus, Menelaus, and the other armed men. At sunset Sinon had given the signal to the fleet waiting at Tenedos, and by morning the Greek ships landed their troops on the shore. There were no guards in sight, as Sinon unlocked the gates.

Six hours later Troy was a smoking ruin. Doors had been battered down, torches hurled into houses; sleeping soldiers were slain before they woke. There was no real resistance. The Trojans were overwhelmed and few escaped. When dawn came, the sun shone on a heap of ruins that once had been a great city. Nothing remained but charred timbers and blackened stones.

The wooden horse had served its purpose. It too had been consumed.

THE RETURN OF ODYSSEUS

... *The Hazardous Homecoming*

LTHOUGH Troy had been destroyed, there was little rejoicing among the victors. The Greeks, wearied by almost ten years of warfare and saddened by the loss of some of their dearest champions, were in no mood to celebrate. They longed only to return home. The leaders separated. Menelaus took his wife, the glorious Helen, back to Sparta. Agamemnon returned to his city of Mycenae. Odysseus, whose stratagem of the wooden horse had ended the war, set sail for his island kingdom of Ithaca. The voyage should have taken a month or two, but it was so filled with incredible obstacles and dangers that it took ten years—as long as the siege of Troy—before he touched the shore of his native land.

Odysseus had never wanted to go to war. He was a kindly king, in love with his wife, Penelope; he was a diplomat and clever statesman rather than a warrior. Besides, there had been a prophecy that if he ever left his home he would not return until twenty years had passed. When the envoys came to persuade him to join the other Greek kings against Troy, the wily Odysseus pretended to be out of his mind. He did mad things, like yoking a horse and an ox together to do his farming. With this unlikely team he began to plow the seashore. "It must be sown," he said, and scattered salt in the plowed-up sand. The envoys suspected he was shamming, so one of them put the king's infant son, Telemachus, in front of the knife-like plow. Odysseus stopped plowing instantly and lifted the child out of the furrow. It was obvious to the envoys that he was not insane, and Odysseus stopped pretending. Bidding goodbye to his anxious wife, he had reluctantly joined the forces against Troy.

31

Now, after a fearful voyage, Odysseus was nearing Ithaca. He had passed through unbelievable adventures, narrowly escaping death again and again.

First, contrary winds had driven him to the coast of Thrace, whose inhabitants were Trojan allies and therefore unfriendly. In a brawl there he had lost several of his crew. Ten days later he came to the Land of the Lotus-Eaters, so called because the inhabitants used the perfumed blossoms, producing blissful forgetfulness, for their food. Here some of the men feasted so happily that they lost all sense of home-going. They would have been content to remain there forever, forsaking the world in easeful dreams, had not Odysseus forced them back to the ships. Then a storm drove them off course, but by good fortune they managed to reach a sheltering island.

This island was the domain of the Cyclopes, monstrous sheep-herding giants with a single eye set in the middle of their foreheads. Finding a convenient cave, Odysseus and twenty of his men took shelter in its depths, not knowing that it belonged to Polyphemus, the most fearsome of his tribe. The cave was stocked with huge bowls of milk, tubs of butter, baskets full of fresh cheese. Making themselves at home, the men helped themselves hungrily until Polyphemus himself arrived, carrying a huge tree to be used for firewood and driving in a flock of sheep the size of oxen. The Cyclops blocked the doors with a flat rock that a team of twenty-four horses could not have budged. As he started to milk the ewes, he spied the men.

"Who are you?" he roared. "And by what right do you enter my home?"

"We are Greeks," answered Odysseus, "and we are trying to reach our own home. We are lost, and if you will aid us you will earn the thanks of the gods, especially Zeus."

"We Cyclopes have no faith in Zeus, or any of the other gods," growled Polyphemus. "We don't need their help, and we don't want their thanks. Where are your ships?"

"Stranded on the shore," said Odysseus. "We ask shelter for only a short time. We will pay for what we ate."

"Oh, you will pay, will you?" And with that he seized two of the men, dashed their heads against the rocky side of the cave, tore away their limbs, roasted them over a fire, ate them, and fell asleep. Odysseus was about to drive his sword into the giant's heart when he remembered the huge rock that served as a closed door. He reflected that even if he killed the monster he and his men could never hope to move the rock. The cave would become their tomb. So he resolved to wait for a better chance to overcome the giant. If he could not outfight him he planned to outwit him.

The next morning Polyphemus made a breakfast of two other men. After drinking a hogshead of milk he drove out the sheep, then replaced the great stone barrier. This happened for two more days. On the third day, while Polyphemus was away, Odysseus found one of the giant's discarded clubs. It was six feet long. Odysseus and his companions cut and smoothed and sharpened it until it was shaped like a huge spear. Then they hid it in a corner and covered it with earth.

When Polyphemus returned at the end of the day, Odysseus offered him some wine his men had brought with them. The giant gulped down three goblets of the heady stuff.

"What do you call yourself," he asked drowsily.

"Call me No-man," said Odysseus.

"Well, No-man, give me another taste of that wine," and before he could finish the goblet, the giant was fast asleep.

This was the moment Odysseus was waiting for. He and four of his men held the long spear-sharp piece of wood in the fire until it was red-hot, then they rammed it into Polyphemus' one eye.

The giant roared, and the noise brought the other Cyclopes to the mouth of the cave.

"What has hurt you?" they asked. "Who did it?"

"No-man," said Polyphemus. "No-man did it."

"If no man did it," they said, "it must have been an accident, or a punishment for something you did." And they left him to his darkness.

Blinded though he was, Polyphemus schemed to lay hold of his assailants. In the morning he rolled back the stone and, certain that the Greeks would now try to escape, stood at the entrance, ready to catch them. Odysseus thought fast. As the huge sheep passed out of the cave, he and his men clung to the thick fleece on the underside of the big animals. Polyphemus ran his hand over the back of each sheep and ram as they went through the opening, never suspecting what the beasts were carrying underneath. Once more Odysseus and his men were saved.

Many other dangers were encountered and obstacles overcome during the years of sea-wandering. There was the floating island of Aeolus whose ruler gave Odysseus a bag containing all the winds, a gift which was to bring him both good fortune and bad. There was the horrible experience with the Laestrygonians, cannibal giants even larger and more ferocious than the Cyclopes, who devoured some of Odysseus' crew and destroyed many of his ships. There was the feverish year on the island of the enchantress Circe, who drugged men with food and wine and then changed them into beasts, a sorceress who enticed the crew but failed to hold Odysseus. There was the time when the north wind brought him close to Hades, where he saw the sufferings of the damned, and barely escaped from the kingdom of perpetual gloom. There was the adventure with the Sirens, whose sweet music would have lured the sailors to destruction had not Odysseus filled the men's ears with wax so that they could not hear the hypnotic singing.

The long journey seemed endless. Much more was to happen to the home-seeking Odysseus. He had to steer his way through a most perilous strait: on one side was Scylla, a six-headed, man-devouring creature with long, serpentine necks and six ferocious mouths; on the other side crouched Charybdis, a hideous monster who created whirlpools that sucked down every ship that came near. After he had lost six men, Odysseus succeeded in making the passage and landing his tired crew on Sicily.

There he was beset by a fresh misfortune. Although warned against touching the cattle sacred to Apollo, the sailors were so hungry that they could not resist killing a few of the herd while Odysseus slept. When he woke, he was horrified to see the hides of the slaughtered oxen creeping painfully along the ground, while the pieces of meat on the spit moaned pitifully. He knew that Apollo would put a curse on those who had committed this sacrilege. Hoping to escape the wrath of the god, he offered a sacrifice and rushed his men to the boats.

But Apollo was not to be appeased so easily. The moment they were embarked, the sky turned black, darkness blotted out the sea, a storm toppled the mast and tore apart the ship's timbers. The beams were so scattered that there was nothing to cling to. All the men were drowned except Odysseus who floated for nine long days and longer nights until he was finally washed up on the shore of an island belonging to the sea-nymph Calypso. Here he was entertained richly and lovingly and, under her spell, he stayed seven years on that delightful island. Calypso wanted to keep him with her forever.

"Stay here," she pleaded with him. "Stay with me, and I will teach you how to enjoy youth forever. You will never grow old. I will give you the greatest of all gifts—I will make you immortal."

But Odysseus could not be persuaded. When she saw how he would sit for hours gazing seawards, she knew that she could not hold him.

"Your heart is elsewhere, I know," she said sadly. "You yearn for what I cannot give you, so I must let you go. I cannot furnish ships or sailors for you, but I can show you where a boat might be built."

She took Odysseus to the other side of her island which was covered by a stand of pine trees. Soon he felled twenty of the tallest pines, cut off the branches, peeled the bark and, lashing the trunks together, made a raft. Calypso watched him tearfully as he renewed his voyage homeward.

Again a storm sprang up, smashed his raft, and almost drowned Odysseus. Clinging to one of the logs, he drifted for days until a favoring wind brought him to shore. Once more he was saved by a lovely woman. Nausicaä, a king's daughter, found him lying exhausted on the sand. She listened to his tale, then brought him to her father. The king was greatly impressed with Odysseus, offered him hospitality of the court, while Nausicaä wished she might have such a man for her husband. But both realized that his one longing was to reach Ithaca. Accordingly, a ship was fitted out for Odysseus and, with an experienced crew, he set sail for Ithaca.

This time the elements were kind. Odysseus slept soundly throughout the journey and, when they reached Ithaca, the sailors, in order not to disturb him, placed him gently on his native soil. Waking, it was some time before Odysseus could be sure where he was. A mist hung over the hills and covered the outlines of the town. He was groping his way through the fog when he stumbled into Eumaeus, his old swineherd. It was no wonder that Eumaeus did not recognize his master. True to the prophecy, Odysseus had been gone exactly twenty years; his face was deeply lined, his hair was a dirty matted gray, his clothes were weather-beaten rags. Nor was Odysseus certain that he wanted to be recognized. Before disclosing himself, he needed to learn what had been happening during his long absence. Resolved to say nothing, he remained overnight at the swineherd's hut.

Daylight brought a young man to the hut. It was Telemachus, Odysseus' son, who had just returned from a futile search for his father and had come to ask Eumaeus for any possible news. Telemachus looked at the stranger; there was something oddly familiar, something almost majestic about the man. Odysseus saw a handsome youth who reminded him of someone, yet he could not recall where he had seen him before. Suddenly the gods gave both men vision. A new light came into Odysseus' eyes, his shoulders straightened, he seemed to grow taller and younger. Every inch proclaimed the king. Telemachus spoke first.

"Are you truly my father?" he said. "Or is it some image conjured up to trick me? Have I traveled everywhere abroad only to find you waiting here?"

"I have not been here long," answered Odysseus, "but truly I am your father. And you are my son." As they embraced, he added, "Now we can go happily home together."

Telemachus did not move. His face darkened.

"You are troubled, my son," said Odysseus. "Is it on my account?"

"On all our accounts," he replied. "There is much you should know, and little time to tell it. We cannot go home now; in fact, we cannot go at all unless we are prepared."

"Prepared for what? You talk mysteriously."

"It is no mystery," said Telemachus. "An absence as long as yours made many believe you had either died at Troy or had perished by shipwreck. Suitors, more than a hundred of them, have come to the palace hoping to marry the rich and lovely lady they believed to be your widow. They made themselves horribly at home. They drank your best wine, feasted themselves on your fattest cattle, sprawled in your palace rooms and slept in your beds. There was no way for my mother to rid herself of them; they came with armed servitors. They ignored her protests and claimed that they were within their rights, that she would have to marry one of them. And whoever she married would occupy your throne."

"How, then," said Odysseus, "did she hold them off?"

"She told them that even if assured of your death, she could not think of another marriage until she had finished weaving a shroud for your father who was very old and would soon die. They were impatient, but they agreed to wait until the work was done before she chose a husband. She was cleverer than they thought. Every day she wove and at night, when the suitors were asleep, she unravelled what she had done. She has been faithful to you through all these years; she never gave up hope that you would return. But now she can put off the time of decision no longer. A few days ago one of the suitors discovered her trick, and told the others.

They were furious. They insisted that she choose one of them for a husband immediately—before nightfall."

"It is indeed a pressing time," Odysseus. "But," he added with a grim smile, "we have a few hours. Let us see what we can do—you and I together—before nightfall."

They talked for an hour or more, suggesting a plan, discarding it, and substituting another. Then, still conversing, father and son came to the palace.

"Don't forget," said Odysseus, "you are to mingle with our uninvited guests as though nothing had happened. If any ask, you will say that there was no news of me, that there seems little likelihood of my being alive anywhere. You will take no notice when I come to the palace in the garb of an old beggar. The laws of hospitality will gain admittance for me without your help. But be ready for the right moment."

Toward the end of day a much-disguised Odysseus entered the courtyard of the palace. No one noticed him except an old dog, Argos, who raised himself on his haunches, wagged his tail, and whined excitedly.

"Lie down, old friend," murmured Odysseus, as he patted his head. "Don't give me away." And he went into the house.

He sat himself in the beggar's seat, on the threshold outside the hall. Telemachus sent a servant with some bread and meat; none of the suitors paid any attention to him except Antinous, the most insolent of them all, who jeered and threw a footstool at him. Odysseus clenched his teeth and rubbed his bruised shoulder; the time to act had not yet come, but it was drawing near. At this moment Penelope sent for the beggar.

"My son tells me you have come from afar," she said. "Perhaps you may have heard tidings about my husband. Although he has been gone for years, I cannot believe he has died. No one is allowed to occupy his seat at the table; his room is always ready for him; his favorite bow is oiled and rubbed every day."

"Your husband is not dead," said Odysseus in a low voice. "I have seen him. When I told him I was headed for Ithaca, he gave me this brooch to show you that he was alive and would not be long returning."

Penelope looked at the brooch which was carved with the figure of a dog and a deer.

"It is his," she said breathlessly. "I remember it well. You bring wonderful news—I do not know how to reward you. Here," she called to his old nurse, Eurycleia. "Tend to the man. He is famished and footsore. See that he is properly clothed and fed. Then bring him to me."

Eurycleia took Odysseus into another room and washed his feet. Noticing a long scar on his thigh, she remembered the day Odysseus had been gored by a wild boar, and cried "You!"

"Hush!" whispered Odysseus, clapping his hand over her mouth. "Not now! Go back, and say nothing to your mistress."

The suitors were still dining when Penelope came into the great hall. Saying that the smoking fireplace had tarnished the shields, spears, and helmets that hung on the wall and that they needed polishing, Telemachus had removed all the weapons from the room except the short swords carried by the suitors.

"I have made up my mind," said Penelope. "In a dream I heard a voice telling me that I should wed the man who could handle my husband's strong bow most skillfully. Odysseus used to set up twelve large axes in a row. These had round holes in their iron heads, and he would shoot an arrow through the twelve openings. I have had the axes set up here. This," she said, indicating the place where it stood, "is the bow."

Antinous was the first to seize the bow. He smiled confidently, then he frowned. He could not bend it. "I have feasted too well," he said. "Let someone else test his strength. I will do it later."

Three more suitors failed; then another three tried, without success. Foolish and shamefaced they shook their heads.

"Will the noble gentlemen permit an old archer to try his hand?" asked Odysseus humbly.

They all jeered. "We must not be rude to the aged," laughed Antinous. "By all means let him try. It should be amusing."

Odysseus took the bow, ran one hand over it lovingly and, with the other, tested the string. He took up an arrow, then, as easily as a musician plucks his harp, twanged the string. The arrow shot through the twelve axe heads, and before the suitors realized what was happening, his rags dropped from him. He stood erect and fitted another arrow into place.

"This is for another target," he said, and shot it through Antinous' throat.

There was a wild uproar. The suitors rushed to arm themselves with shields, spears, and helmets, but the bare walls mocked them. They ran to the door. There stood Telemachus, with a few of the palace guards, fully armed. The turmoil increased, but the struggle

was short. Swinging their swords in groups of threes and fours, the suitors flung themselves toward Odysseus. One by one he picked them off. Those who tried to escape were cut down by Telemachus and the guards. The violence continued until the last of the suitors perished and the floor was littered with the slain.

Not until the bodies were removed and the hall washed clean did the hero draw a deep breath. Not until then did he look at his son still standing in the doorway and at his wife who had remained transfixed with fear and wonder. After the cries and the clashing of swords the room was strangely still. The world-weary traveler sank into his old, accustomed seat.

Odysseus had come home.

THE RACE FROM MARATHON

...*The Heroic Runner*

wo hundred years before the great Alexander con-
quered most of the world for Greece, Darius I of
Persia created an empire that stretched across two
continents. He invaded Egypt, where he super-
vised what was then an amazing feat: the digging
of a canal from the Nile to the Red Sea. He penetrated India and founded new colonies there; he built royal resi-
dences in such glamorous places as Persepolis, Ecbatana, Susa, and
Babylon. Having established a foothold in the Greek province of
Asia Minor, and controlling the sea, he threatened to add Greece
to his vast empire. To all the Greek states he sent envoys, demand-
ing that they surrender and deliver to the envoys a tribute of earth
and water as symbols to show that the land and the sea belonged
to Persia.

Two states resisted: Eretria and Athens. The Eretrians refused to
receive the envoys and pelted them with earth and water. The
Athenians showed their independent spirit even more decisively:
they bound the envoys and threw them in a muddy ditch, telling
them, "Here's earth and water for you and your master!"

Darius determined to punish the resisters. "Show no mercy to
the rebels," he told his generals. "Athens and Eretria must be enslaved. Then bring the slaves into my presence."

Eretria was besieged first and, frightened by the huge Persian
army, the Eretrians not only surrendered but agreed to flash sig-
nals to the invaders with their shields as soon as an Athenian army
was encamped on the plain at Marathon, twenty-two miles from
Athens. The Persians sent a fleet to Marathon. There they planned

to engage the Athenians between the flooded marshes and the low-lying hills.

The great general Miltiades was in charge of the Athenian troops. With Greek reinforcements, his army occupied the passes covering the road to Athens. Miltiades sent one of his regiments out in a clever flanking movement to prevent a Persian breakthrough. The Persians found themselves pinned down. Most of the combined Greek army was in a narrow valley enclosed by high cliffs, and the Persian cavalry, ordinarily so effective, knew they would be cut to pieces if they rode into that narrow defile.

Darius decided to withdraw his horsemen and most of his foot soldiers. But, before he could put the plan into operation, Miltiades acted. Seeing that Darius had weakened his line, Miltiades sent his bronze-armored men streaming out of the passes. For a while the Persians stood fast, hurling their missiles; but, though the Athenians were outnumbered six to one, their courageous charge proved overwhelming, and Darius was forced to retreat. More than six thousand Persians lost their lives, while the Greek losses were less than two hundred.

The Greek general called on his courier, Pheidippides.

"Carry the news to Athens as fast as you can. No horses are available. You will have to go on foot. Tell them of the victory, but warn them that Darius still has ships, and the city should be prepared."

Pheidippides ran. He ran the twenty-two miles from the battlefield to Athens. His heart pounded ominously, but he never stopped. A dozen arms reached out to keep him from falling when, with his last breath, he lurched through the city gates.

"Rejoice!" he gasped. "The victory is ours! Rejoice—but prepare!" The Athenians shouted for joy. He died in their arms.

More than two thousand years later, Pheidippides was honored by the entire world. In 1896 the first modern long distance marathon race was held at the revival of the Olympic games in Athens. Athletes from every nation participated, and the stadium burst into cheers when the victor was announced. By a happy coincidence the marathon race had been won by a Greek runner.

THE PASS AT THERMOPYLAE

...The Fearless Three Hundred

 HOUGH Darius I, king of Persia, had been defeated at Marathon, he did not give up his intention of conquering Greece. But, in the midst of preparations for a new campaign, Darius died. He was succeeded by his son, Xerxes, who inherited not only his father's throne but his determination to bring Greece under Persian rule.

Xerxes started his expedition with what seemed a million men. There were actually more than three hundred thousand trained soldiers and they made their way through Thrace and Macedonia, supported by the largest fleet in the world. In the late summer of 481 B. C. they reached the Hellespont, where Xerxes ordered a great number of flat boats to be lashed together across the straits. It took seven days and seven nights for his army to pass over this bridge of boats.

Once on Greek soil, Xerxes, like Darius, sent demands to the cities of Greece for tributes of earth and water, the symbols of submission. Again the demand was rejected. Refusing to be slaves, the Greeks resolved to defend themselves and preserve their proud spirit of freedom. The Persian army reached the pass of Thermopylae (literally the Hot Gates because of the hot sulphur springs nearby) burning and destroying as they advanced.

The Greeks had been warned of Xerxes' approach, and a few thousand troops were waiting for him. Though greatly outnumbered by the Persian hordes, they were untroubled. They were camped securely in the narrowest sort of defile, a place where two or three armed men could hold a company at bay. Except for a secret concealed path over the mountain, there was no way of getting through, and this path was guarded by men from the city of Phocis. Unaware of the secret mountain path, Xerxes wanted to learn how many men were holding the pass at Thermopylae and what they were doing. He dispatched a spy to find out.

"Your majesty," the spy reported, "there are only a few thousand, but they are led by the Spartan king, Leonidas, and the Spartans are a stubborn, foolhardy lot. They care nothing about risking their lives. It is said that they celebrate their own funeral rites before they go to war. Even the women, they say, when they bid their men farewell, tell them to return either carrying their shields or being carried on them. They also say——"

Xerxes cut him short.

"They say! They say! What does it matter what they say! The important thing is that the Greeks—Spartans and all—are outnumbered a hundred to one. I also sent you to learn something else. What were the troops doing?"

"They were combing their hair," said the spy.

"What!" exclaimed Xerxes. He did not know that the Spartans always combed their hair just before going into battle, to make their heavy helmets fit better. He assumed that they were frivolous. "They sound more like silly women than fighting men. We will show them what fighting really means." And he gave the order to attack.

The first wave of Persian troops came at dawn. A vast number of archers led the charge.

"Look!" said Leonidas' second-in-command: "How many they are! When they shoot, their arrows darken the sun!"

"Good," said Leonidas. "We can fight better in the shade."

The arrows came down in a dense cloud, but the Greek helmets and shields warded them off, while the long Greek spears caused havoc among the Persians. Another cohort of Persians were thrown against the Greeks, and again they were repulsed. For three days column after column of Persian troops stormed the pass, but the Greeks held firm. Xerxes was furious. He called on his picked troops known as the Ten Thousand Immortals.

"Prove your immortality," he commanded them. "Go in and wipe out that little group so eager to die."

But the Immortal Ten Thousand fared no better than the others; they too were beaten off. Legend has it that the mighty Xerxes raged with anger and terror like a hysterical child, jumping up and down on his throne.

That night a man was brought to Xerxes' tent. It was Ephialtes, a Greek, who was ready to turn traitor and reveal a secret—for a large sum of money.

"I will buy your secret," said Xerxes, "if you can prove it is worth anything."

"It is worth your army," said Ephialtes. "I can prove it. The pass of Thermopylae is not the only way through. There is a footpath over the mountain that leads to the rear of the Greeks. It is held by only a handful of soldiers; they are not Spartans but Phocians, men who would rather live than die. A quick attack, and you can surprise Leonidas on the other side."

"You have proved nothing yet," said Xerxes.

"Give me a hundred of your soldiers and I will prove it tonight. I will lead them to the place. If I succeed, you will pay me well; if I fail, you will have my head."

Ephialtes succeeded. He guided a Persian company up the secret side path to the highest point. It was a windy autumn night, and the Phocian defenders did not realize until too late that what they thought was the rustle of fallen leaves was the scuffle of feet. They were easily routed. But, before they retreated into the depths of the wooded mountain, they managed to get word to Leonidas. He called a meeting of his captains in the middle of the night.

"Our position has changed," he told them grimly. "There is no way by which we can give battle in the open. We have been facing a hugely superior force in front; we are now going to be trapped in the rear. We cannot possibly defeat Xerxes, but we can delay him. We can keep him here and weaken him while the Athenians strengthen their defenses and prepare ships to oppose the Persian fleet. We have already held him for more than three days. We can hold him a few days more in this pass, and for that we need only a small force. I am sending most of you back to your cities. You will not be needed; you can slip through the woods. The Spartans will stay with me."

The captains protested, but they had to obey. When the rest of the Greeks withdrew, Leonidas was left with his three hundred Spartans. The odds against him now were a thousand to one.

Leonidas dressed himself in his royal robe, performed the final sacrifice as king, then disrobed and put on his armor. He would die with his men as a Spartan warrior, not as a ruler.

For three days the Spartans held the enemy. The Persians came forward fearfully and resentfully. Many of them were forced into combat with whips; those who lagged were trampled underfoot by troops driven from behind. But their tremendous superiority in numbers meant inevitable success. The Spartans fought desperately, shoulder to shoulder. They fought with swords until the blades snapped; then they used daggers; when these were gone, they fought with their hands. Leonidas was one of the last to succumb. He died on a mound of his slain men at the mouth of the pass.

Xerxes had won the battle at a tremendous cost. He had won the battle, but he had not won the war. When he reached Athens, thanks to the delay at Thermopylae, the city was deserted. As the Persian fleet sailed out to ensure Xerxes' land victory, it was met by the reinforced Greek ships. In the great naval encounter at Salamis, the Persians were thoroughly defeated.

At the opening of the pass at Thermopylae a monument was raised, and on it a brief verse was inscribed in memory of the three hundred who made their brave stand there:

> Pause, traveler, ere you go your way. Then tell
> How, Spartan to the last, we fought and fell.

A SPARTAN REPLY

...*The Laconic Answer*

 ING Philip of Macedon, father of Alexander the Great, had won so many victories and had captured so much territory that everyone expected him to invade Greece. This he planned to do, but he hesitated because of the Spartans.

The Spartans lived in that part of Greece known as Laconia. A brave and simple people, utterly fearless, they were not given to boasting or vain talk. They used few words and chose those words carefully; their sentences were so short that they were called "laconic," a form of speech native to Laconia.

Philip at last decided that he would wait no longer. Assembling a vast army, he brought it to the borders of Laconia. Then he sent a message to the Spartans.

"When I invade your country," he warned them, "if you do not yield at once, I will burn your villages and destroy your cities. If I enter Laconia I will level it to the ground."

The Spartans did not waste words or time. Their answer came back immediately, a truly laconic reply. It consisted of a single word.

The word was "IF!"

BUCEPHALUS

...Alexander's Kingly Horse

VEN as a young boy Prince Alexander, son of Philip of Macedon, acted like a king. He bore himself proudly, he dressed in regal robes, and seemed to wear an invisible crown long before he became Alexander the Great. Once at a festival of Greek games, his father, knowing he was a swift runner, asked him if he would like to compete in the foot races.

"No," said Alexander. "The other runners are ordinary men. I race only with kings."

Arrogant though he was with people, Alexander was kind and gentle with animals. A skilled horseman by the time he was twelve, he was particularly fond of horses and understood their many moods. One day he was standing at his father's side when a groom displayed a new purchase, a handsome black stallion that Philip had just bought.

"A noble animal," said Philip, "I've never seen a more magnificent creature."

"Yes," said Alexander. "He looks like the king of horses." The groom said nothing.

"Why are you frowning?" Philip asked the groom. "Is there anything wrong with him?"

"Nothing except one thing, your majesty," answered the groom. "His name is Bucephalus, which means 'bull-headed,' you know, and his nature is like his name. He is, as you say, a fine-looking beast, and he's docile enough when being led around as I am doing now. But let anyone try to mount him, and he becomes a wild bull. Coaxing does no good; whipping only makes him worse. He will permit no one to stay on his back."

"Let us see," said Philip. "Surely, among all my men, there should be a few who can ride this black beauty."

Men were sent for, men from the stable, expert horsemen, veteran hunters, members of the cavalry. None could succeed in curbing the fiery spirit of Bucephalus. The moment he felt a hand on his neck and a foot swung over his side, he snorted and reared, kicked his heels high in the air, pranced and plunged, and threw off anyone attempting to mount him.

Alexander had been watching the horse's actions. "Let me try him," he said.

Philip smiled. "I allow you to do many things, my son. But do you think I should let you risk your life with this fierce fellow? Do you think you can succeed where my best riders have failed?"

"Yes, father. I think I can succeed," said Alexander. "I know that horse already—I know him better than he knows himself."

"I suppose I must let you try," said Philip. "I don't believe he will throw you too hard. In fact, since he won't let you on his back, you may not be thrown at all. If, however, you should manage to stay on him for more than a minute, he is yours."

Alexander walked slowly to where Bucephalus was standing. The horse pawed the ground, looking suspiciously at the figure coming near him. Alexander had noticed that the horse seemed to shy away from his own shadow. The sun was strong, and the black shadow in front of him seemed like another horse that kicked and reared even more furiously than Bucephalus himself.

"Come," whispered Alexander to Bucephalus. "There's nothing to frighten you," and he gently turned the horse's head toward the sun until he could not see the shadow lying behind him. Then lightly he leaped upon his back.

Bucephalus trembled, but Alexander ran his hands comfortingly over his neck as he talked to him and caressed him. Slowly the boy guided the great horse around the field. Once, twice, and three times they circled. Now Alexander gave the horse an urging pat, and Bucephalus broke into a trot, then a canter, then they were off at a gallop. When Alexander reined him in, Bucephalus whinnied with pleasure. He sensed this was a master to be proud of, and that his master was proud of him.

"See, father," cried Alexander, quivering with excitement. "I told you he was the king of horses!"

From that day on Alexander and Bucephalus were inseparable. And when Bucephalus died, Alexander had him buried with pomp and ceremony, and grieved as one grieves for the loss of a dear friend.

THE GORDIAN KNOT

...And How It Was Untied

ORDIUS was a poor farmer who lived in the country of Phrygia, in Asia Minor. He was poor in every sense: poor in his land, poor in property and poor in health. With one cart and one team of oxen, it was all he could do just to plow and plant the rocky soil which yielded him so little.

One spring day when he was making a furrow for beans, an eagle swooped down from the sky. At first Gordius thought the bird of prey was going to attack the oxen. "There's not enough beef on their bones for a decent meal," he said half to himself, half to the eagle. But the great bird merely floated toward Gordius, perched upon the plow, folded its powerful wings, and sat there.

Gordius was greatly disturbed. "Surely this means something," he thought. "It must be some kind of portent, perhaps a message from the gods. But what can it mean? I must find someone who can interpret this omen, if that's what it is."

The next morning Gordius set out for the temple of Zeus that stood in the chief city of Phrygia. He had never been there before. He knew nothing of city ways or city life; he did not even know that there had been a civil war and that Phrygia had been without a king for some years. After much fighting, and much bloodshed about who should rule the land, the people had still come to no decision. Finally they sent to the oracle of Apollo for guidance. The answer had just arrived.

"The lowliest thing shall be the highest," it ran. "The father shall turn the neediest into the mightiest."

It was an impressive saying, but as an answer no one could understand it. Not until poor Gordius drove into the city, told about the eagle's omen, and asked to be directed to the temple of Zeus did the townspeople begin to say that the oracle's message might not remain a mystery.

"He is certainly the lowliest-looking thing ever to enter the city," said one.

"Nothing is needier than a farmer whose poor oxen can barely drag his cart," said another. "But what has that to do with a father?"

"Let's take him to the temple of Zeus," said the first man, who seemed to be a person of some authority. "Perhaps the priest can explain."

After Gordius had told his story, the priest said, "Come back at nightfall. First I must meditate. Then, after the evening sacrifice, I may unravel the meaning of all this."

When Gordius returned he was trailed by a great crowd that poured into the temple. The priest raised his hands high above his head and addressed them.

"The god has spoken. What Gordius saw was not only an omen but also a prophecy. The oracle of Apollo and the eagle perched on the plow mean the same thing. The eagle is the bird who sits at the right hand of Zeus, and Zeus is the father of Apollo. Both messages tell us that we who have been so proud must learn from the humble—'the lowliest thing shall be the highest.' And who is lowlier than this poor farmer? The oracle also said: 'The father shall turn the neediest into the mightiest'—which means it is the will of Zeus, the father god, that we, who have been looking in vain for a ruler, have found him. No one in Phrygia is needier than this man."

So Gordius the farmer became Gordius the king. He ruled wisely and mercifully for many years, for he knew the needs of the simple, plain people. His cart was placed near the altar of Zeus, and before he died Gordius fastened the ox-yoke to a beam of the temple with stout cords and tied it in such a complicated knot that they could not be loosened. Hundreds of Phrygians and every visitor to the city tried, but no one could untie the cords. The knot seemed to grow tighter with time. People regarded the thing with something like awe. There grew to be a saying:

"The man who can untie the Gordian knot will rule not only Phrygia but the world."

A hundred years passed. After the death of his father, Alexander had become king of Macedon. He outdid the mighty Philip as ruler and warrior. He invaded Thebes on the mainland of Greece, and went on to subdue the other Greek states. Crossing the Hellespont, he landed in Asia Minor near the plain of ancient Troy, and

routed the powerful Persian army. After invading Egypt, he founded a lordly city there, and called it Alexandria. He won victory after victory; his achievements matched his ambition which was endless.

He was still in his twenties when he came to Phrygia. There he was shown the cart of Gordius in the temple of Jupiter. He smiled.

"I know about this remarkable knotted wonder," he said, "and I have heard the famous saying." He drew his sword. "This is how Alexander unties the Gordian knot." And with one swift stroke he cut the knot into shreds.

The saying turned out to be right, the prophecy was fulfilled. Alexander the Great went on to rule not only Phrygia but the world. Even then his ambition was not satisfied. Alexander wept because there were no more worlds to conquer.

DIOGENES

... *The Simple Life*

IOGENES was one of the world's wisest men. It has been said that poets are born, not made. No man, however, is born wise; wisdom is something that has to be acquired.

Diogenes was no exception. He was a bright boy from Corinth who wanted to be brighter. In Athens there was a noted teacher and, when he was seventeen, Diogenes went to him for instruction.

"Teach me how to become a wise man," said Diogenes.

"Go home, young man," said the teacher. "Wisdom is something you have to learn from experience. Besides, I have too many older pupils to bother with anyone as young as you."

"I came here to learn," persisted Diogenes. "And here I will stay until I have been taught something."

"I'll teach you not to be impertinent," said the teacher, and picking up his staff he struck Diogenes several sharp blows.

Diogenes did not run away; he did not even flinch. "Keep on striking me," he said. "I intend to stay as long as I can learn something. And I already have learned that a man who teaches others to be calm and controlled can lose his temper."

"I am properly rebuked," said the teacher. "Come to class tomorrow. I can see you will be one of my best pupils."

Diogenes learned rapidly. He learned from teachers, from books, from all sorts of people, from great events and small happenings, from the most important and the least significant details of daily life. Then *he* began to teach. People came from great distances to hear him speak.

He spoke mostly about simplicity, about how our bodies are

56

stuffed with too much food and how our lives are softened and spoiled by too many pleasures and indulgences.

"We should learn to live without luxuries," he preached. "We should give up everything except what is truly necessary, and find comfort in little things, in next to nothing."

He impressed people not only because of his philosophy, but also because he practiced what he preached. He ate the simplest foods, chiefly raw vegetables, berries, and nuts; he refused to live in a house but made his home in a barrel-shaped tub which he rolled from one sunny spot to another.

Simplicity was the keynote of his talks. Sometimes he talked about one other thing he said was equally rare in the world: honesty.

One day the townspeople were startled to see Diogenes walking in the middle of the day carrying a lighted lantern.

"What are you seeking?" someone asked. "And why are you carrying a lantern in daylight?"

"I am looking for an honest man," said Diogenes. "It takes more than ordinary light to find one."

Diogenes envied no man. He asked nothing of anyone; he needed nothing. A contented man, he was at home with himself and the world.

When Alexander the Great came to Corinth, everyone flocked to do homage to him—everyone except Diogenes. Alexander had heard of the famous scholar and was anxious to hear what wisdom he might dispense.

"If the great Diogenes will not come to the great Alexander," he said, "then Alexander must visit Diogenes."

He found the philosopher sitting in front of his barrel. Diogenes was meditating in the warmth of the spring morning.

"Your reputation has reached me across the seas," said Alexander. "Mine must have reached you too, and you must know that there is no favor I cannot grant. Now tell me, is there something I can do for you?"

"Yes, there is," replied Diogenes. "Move aside. You are standing in my sunlight."

ARCHIMEDES

... *Eureka!*

IKE Diogenes, Archimedes was a philosopher. Unlike Diogenes, Archimedes relished the good things of life. He lived during the third century B. C. in the wealthy city of Syracuse on the island of Sicily and was a frequent guest in the homes of the very rich, as well as the royal household. His best friend was Hiero, King of Syracuse.

Hiero loved splendor. He owned the finest horses in the land, built the largest palace, and sat on the most elaborate throne. To celebrate his birthday he ordered a new and magnificent crown. He designed it himself.

"This is the way it must look," he told the court jeweler. "Heavy, but not uncomfortable to wear. Not gaudy—no jewels, you understand—but beautiful because of its massive purity. That is why I am giving you this block of pure gold. Use every grain of it, and have it ready for me within a month."

A month later the crown was ready. Hiero was a little suspicious of the jeweler. He had seen to it that the gold was weighed before he gave it to him. The gold had weighed exactly ten pounds. He weighed the crown when it arrived. It, too, weighed ten pounds. Yet there was something about the crown that dissatisfied the king. It was large enough, a little too large in fact, and the color was good, although somehow disappointing. Something about the crown troubled him, something he could not define even to himself. He called in Archimedes who, besides being a philosopher, was also a mathematician and scientist.

"Something seems to be wrong with the crown," said Hiero. "Look at this ten-pound lump of pure gold and then look at the crown."

Archimedes examined them carefully.

"For one thing," he said, "the color is not quite the same. The lump of gold has a reddish color while the crown looks both brighter and yellower. This, of course, could have happened in the melting and molding. Then there's the matter of size. You tell me that the two objects weigh the same, yet the crown seems bulkier than it should. Is it possible the jeweler cheated by keeping some of the gold and adding silver to make up the difference in weight? Silver is much lighter than gold, you know. So he would have had to put in quite a lot of silver when he alloyed the gold—if that is what he did do."

"Is there any way of finding out?" asked Hiero.

"None that I know of," answered Archimedes. "It's a puzzle. But let me think about it."

He continued to think about a possible test without coming to any conclusion. Then one day the answer came in a most curious way. Stepping into his bath, Archimedes did not notice that the tub had been filled to the brim. When he sat down in it, the water ran over and poured out on the floor.

"This must have happened to me before, but I paid no attention to it," he said to himself. "Now I see its importance. My body going into the water has forced a certain amount out of this tub. Let's see now——a larger man would displace more water, a smaller man less. The greater the volume, the greater the displacement. Why wouldn't this apply to everything—even to Hiero's crown? Silver is lighter than gold; therefore a pound of silver will have more bulk than a pound of gold. If the crown still has the same amount of gold that was in the original block, then both will displace the same amount of water. But suppose it's part silver——then, in order to weigh the same, it would have to be bulkier. In a test, it would take up more space and force out more water than pure gold."

Excited by his discovery, Archimedes leaped from the tub and, throwing a towel about him, rushed through the streets to the palace shouting "Eureka! Eureka"——which is Greek for "I have found it! I have found it!"

Hiero was almost as excited as the philosopher-scientist. They decided to test Archimedes' discovery at once. A ten-pound lump of gold was placed in a bowl of water that was not quite full. It brought the water to the brim, but not a drop spilled over. Then the crown was placed in the same bowl. The water flowed over the top.

When summoned, the jeweler threw himself at the king's feet and confessed. Some historians tell that the dishonest craftsman was stoned to death with lumps of his own silver. Others are more merciful. They say that Hiero was so delighted with the discovery that he pardoned the culprit and gave the crown to Archimedes.

CROESUS

...The World's Richest Man

 ROESUS was King of Lydia more than two thousand and five hundred years ago. He was king in name only; his ministers ruled the country, for Croesus was not interested in affairs of state. He had only one interest: wealth. He collected magnificent things from every nation—gorgeous tapestries, deep velvet carpets, wonderfully carved furniture, silks so delicate they seemed woven from cobwebs, precious painted vases, rare jewels, bowls of silver and goblets of gold. By the time he was thirty he had realized his ambition. He was the richest man in the world. When people wanted to express the very limits of wealth they would say "as rich as Croesus."

He was overjoyed when Solon visited Lydia. Solon was not only Greece's greatest law-giver but a beloved sage; the highest praise a man could receive was to be called "as wise as Solon." The richest man was glad to show the wisest man his treasures. Croesus conducted his guest through the sumptuous rooms, calling his attention to one superb object after another. Solon smiled, murmured, but said nothing in particular. Croesus was determined to make Solon admit he was impressed.

"A man cannot help but be proud of such possessions," he said. "They gladden the heart as well as the eye. I hate to boast, but tell me, Solon, who would you say has the right to call himself the happiest of men?"

Solon thought a moment. Then he replied. "A poor man I knew who lived in Athens. His name was Tellus."

Croesus could not hide his disappointment. "A poor man?" he said. "What made him so happy?"

"His life was rich even though he himself was not. His life was blessed with happiness and honor. Tellus worked hard and brought up five children who became fine citizens. He had no envy, no meanness, no enemies, and he died gloriously defending his country."

Croesus swallowed hard. Then he smiled and asked, "And who do you consider the second happiest man you ever met?"

"I would have to name two men," replied Solon. "Two brothers, Brito and Cleobis. They lived in Argos. They, too, were workers, but they were also athletes who had won prizes in foot races. They were devoted to their invalid mother and, since their father had died when they were children, they kept house for her and worked constantly for her comfort. One year, when the time came for their competition in the annual games, the oxen took sick. The two brothers put themselves in harness and, placing their mother in the cart, pulled it fifty miles to the festival. They were the most praised citizens of Argos—and the happiest."

"So you believe that labor is what makes a man happy?" asked the baffled Croesus.

Solon smiled again. "Not labor alone," he said. "Labor—and love. No one can be called happy until he has lived his life to the full. Know yourself. No man can tell, until the end, whether his good fortune will continue or whether misfortune will some day overtake him."

Croesus did not like this way of thinking; he was uncomfortable until Solon left. Then he forgot about the sage and was thoughtlessly happy again.

A few years later the first misfortune overtook Croesus. There had been a prophecy that one of his sons would die of a weapon wound, so Croesus had forbidden the boy ever to carry arms. Instead of weapons he was given pets of many kinds. One day he was walking in the forest with his favorite hound when the dog spotted a deer and gave chase. The boy ran after him. At that moment, a hunter, seeing the leaping animal, cast his spear. It missed the deer but hit the boy. He died instantly.

Croesus was still mourning for the loss of his son when he received another shock. His kingdom was threatened with invasion by Cyrus the Great, founder of the Persian empire. Croesus, who had given no thought to government, was faced with the possibility of a disastrous war. He decided to consult the oracle at Delphi.

Unlike many of the vague replies, the answer this time seemed clear.

"If you make the proper sacrifice," the oracle prophesied, "an empire will fall."

Croesus made an offering to the gods and summoned his generals. War was declared. But the troops had received little training and there was no preparation for an emergency. The Persian army swept over the border, crushed the weak resistance, and captured not only the capital city but Croesus himself. Croesus realized too late that the sacrifice suggested was not a temple offering, but the sacrifice of his wealth, and that the empire prophesied to fall was not the Persian empire but his own.

His army was disbanded, his gorgeous palace destroyed, and all his treasures confiscated. Croesus himself was dragged to the center of the ruined city. A strong piece of timber was set up, a heap of dry wood piled around it, and Croesus was tied to the stake. Bleeding and bewildered, he thought of Solon's words: "No man can know, until the end, whether his good fortune will continue or whether misfortune will overtake him."

"Oh, Solon!" he wept. "Oh, Solon!"

By good instead of bad fortune, Cyrus happened to be riding by just as a soldier was about to put a torch to the pile.

"Who is it that calls upon the wise law-giver at such a time?" he asked. Then he recognized Croesus. And Croesus told Cyrus about Solon's visit, what he had told him, and how a king had been too proud and too foolish to try to understand wisdom.

Cyrus began to think how the words might also affect him, the greatest living ruler, as well as the miserable prisoner about to die. "Misfortune could overtake me, too," he said to himself. "My happiness in this victory may not last. There are accidents and enemies. No man can know until the end."

Then he spoke to the soldiers. "Untie that man," he said. "Croesus travels with me."

THE SWORD OF DAMOCLES

... *The Man Who Wanted to be King*

IONYSIUS was the ruler of Syracuse, the richest city in Sicily. He had become its absolute master by a combination of shrewd judgment, hard work, and good luck. He knew when to flatter friends and when to placate enemies, when to be kind and when to be ruthless. Many hated him for his success and his power; numerous plans were discussed for his overthrow. There were plotters and schemers in his own household. In spite of everything, Dionysius continued to hold supreme power. Although his fellow-townsmen envied him they were proud to call him the Tyrant of Syracuse.

One of the most envious was Damocles, who was Dionysius' closest friend. He longed to enjoy the ruler's lavish manner of living. Most of all, he envied him his power.

"You must be the happiest man in the world," Damocles kept saying. "There is no man as fortunate as you."

One day Dionysius stopped him in the midst of his praises. "What makes you think I'm so blessed with happiness?" he inquired.

"You must be," replied Damocles. "You have everything that anyone could desire. You are a powerful ruler, you have enormous wealth, you live like a king."

Dionysius smiled. "Would you like to change places with me?"

"That thought never occurred to me," said Damocles. "I wouldn't presume to think, even to dream, of such a thing."

"Well," said Dionysius, "think of it now. Come, change places with me, at least for a trial. You say I live like a king. Live that way, too—be king for a day."

Damocles was easily persuaded; he had already persuaded himself. The next day he put on his best attire and went to the palace. Acting upon instructions from Dionysius the guards saluted him, a welcoming group of girls crowned him with a wreath of gold and put perfumed garlands about his neck. The day was spent luxuriously: nothing to do but listen to music, play games, watch dances, and delight in one entertainment after another. Finally evening came. Damocles was attired in royal robes, and escorted to the dining hall. He sat at the head of the table, while Dionysius, like a not too important guest, sat at the foot.

It was a memorable repast. Damocles was served such delicacies as pearl oysters, tiny crabs in a delicious sauce, and a sugar-coated pie which, when opened, released a dozen singing thrushes. This was accompanied by the smoothest wines, followed by mysteriously flavored ices and tropical fruit. Hundreds of candles lighted up brilliant tapestries while soft music and aromatic incense filled the room. Never had Damocles enjoyed himself so completely. Smiling, he lifted his wine cup in thanks to Dionysius, and Dionysius smiled back.

As he lifted the cup, Damocles raised his eyes. Then his body stiffened. He sat frozen with fear. Directly above his head there hung a sword. The blade glittered; its point was only six or seven inches above his head. It was held by a single thread. Damocles started to rise, but stopped himself, afraid that a sudden motion might break the slender thread and bring the sword down on his head. He stifled a shriek and, trembling, put down his cup ever so carefully.

"Now, what can possibly be startling you?" asked Dionysius placidly. "Is there anything unusual?"

"The sword! The sword!" whispered Damocles through teeth that chattered violently. "Don't you see it?"

"Of course I see it," answered Dionysius. "I have always seen it. There is a sword above the head of every king or ruler, of every one in power. What is worse, it is a sword that may fall at any moment. It hangs by the frailest of threads, and there is always someone ready to cut that thread. If you want to be a ruler, that is something you must learn to live with."

"Thank you," said Damocles, "I have already learned the lesson."

He rose from the head of the table. "Please take your rightful seat," he said to Dionysius, "I will never again want to change places with you—or with anyone else. Never."

DAMON AND PYTHIAS

... *The Perfect Friendship*

 LTHOUGH Dionysius was known as the Tyrant of Syracuse—a name applied in ancient Greece to any absolute ruler who had usurped his power—he was not really cruel or cold-hearted. However, he was easily offended, and when he was annoyed he lost his temper and was much too severe with those who had offended him.

Pythias, a young scholar, had displeased the ruler because of his public speeches. When, together with his friend Damon, he was brought before Dionysius he did not bow low as the king's subjects were in the habit of doing but stood facing the monarch with head held high.

"Don't you know you are supposed to bend the knee and ask my pardon for what you have done?" said Dionysius.

"I've done nothing of which I'm ashamed," said Pythias. "My school teaches that all men are equal and that no man should have absolute power over any other man."

"What school is that which holds such views?" asked Dionysius, beginning to lose his temper.

"The school of the philosopher Pythagoras," replied Pythias.

"It is treason to spread such a philosophy. It has been reported you say that kings have too much power, that their acts can be unwise and their laws unjust."

"That is true. It is also true that I am not afraid of being punished," said Pythias. "My school teaches patience."

"Your school!" said Dionysius angrily. "Very well, we shall put it to the test. We shall see how patient you can be. You will be imprisoned, and you will be given exactly one month to change your

68

views. If you are still stubborn at the end of that time you will be
sentenced to die. Have you anything more to say?"

"I have a request. Permit me to go to my home, put my affairs in
order, and make arrangements for my mother and father."

Dionysius laughed scornfully. "Do you take me for a fool! Once
I let you leave Syracuse, you will never return."

"I will guarantee my return," said Pythias.

"What sort of guarantee can you possibly give?" asked Dionysius.

Damon, who up to that moment had stood by silently, spoke.

"O king," he said. "I will be his guarantee. Pythias and I have
been best friends since our boyhood. We are members of the same
school. Let me take his place in prison. I know that Pythias will
never break a promise."

Dionysius was startled. "That is all very fine," he said. "But any
man who takes the place of a prisoner is subject to the same penalty
as the prisoner himself. Suppose that, in spite of your confidence,
your friend fails to return and he receives the sentence of death——
what then?"

"Then," said Damon calmly, "I will die in his stead."

"Well and good," said Dionysius to Damon. "I will accept the
offer. But I warn you, if your friend doesn't return within a month
from today, your life will not be spared. Now," he said, turning to
the guards, "take him away."

Damon was imprisoned in a sunken chasm, one of those open
caverns in the rocks peculiar to Syracuse. The most famous one was
—and still is—called the Ear of Dionysius because the amazing
acoustics made it possible for the Tyrant, standing above, to catch
any plotting, even the faintest whisper, among the prisoners below.
Dionysius went often to the Ear, but if he expected that Damon
would fret or weep or cry for mercy, he was much mistaken. Never
a word of complaint came from his sunken prison.

Two weeks went by, yet Damon showed no signs of worry. Some
of his fellow prisoners mocked him for his folly; others sympathized
with him. But Damon remained confident.

"He has been delayed—he has had trouble on the road or he has
met with an accident. But I have faith in my friend. He will be
here in time; there is nothing to fear."

Another two weeks passed and there was still no sign of Pythias.
On the last day, Damon was brought out of his cell. His hands were
bound and he was taken to the place of execution.

"What have you to say now?" sneered Dionysius. "Do you still believe in the noble words of your friend?"

"I believe what he believes," answered Damon. "And I believe in him."

As if in proof of these words, Pythias suddenly rushed in. His clothes were torn, his face was haggard, he could scarcely hold himself erect.

"Thank the gods I am here," he gasped. "Everything has been against me. My ship was wrecked on the way out, and later I was captured by robbers. But I did not lose my faith—and fate brought me back in time. Let me receive the sentence."

"The sentence of death is revoked," said Dionysius. "Neither of you shall die. Never have I witnessed such faith, such trust and loyalty. I am rebuked. I would exchange all my ministers and counsellors for one such man as either Damon or Pythias."

Then, after a pause, he said, "Let me, in turn, ask a favor."

"What kind of favor?" inquired the two friends.

"Let me be the third in this friendship," said Dionysius.

THE TWO PAINTERS

...Real or Unreal?

 EUXIS and Parrhasius were artists who were such good friends that they were often called the Damon and Pythias of painting. But, besides being friends, they were rivals. Each boasted that he could outdo the other in his work. Zeuxis argued that art was greater than nature, while Parrhasius claimed that nature *was* the greatest form of art.

"Let us stop arguing," said Zeuxis one day. "Let us put our paintings to the test. Art and nature—it does not matter which is superior. Our task is to paint so well that we can make what is unreal seem real."

"I agree," said Parrhasius. "You shall paint a picture, and I will pass judgment on it. Then I will make a painting, and you shall be the judge."

A week later Zeuxis called on Parrhasius to see the finished work. "Sit here in the garden," he said, "while I bring out the picture. Then we may judge what is real and what is unreal."

In a few minutes Zeuxis brought out a medium-size painting of a bowl of fruit. The peaches looked as if they had just been picked; the cherries were bursting with sweetness; a drop of morning dew shone on a purple plum.

Zeuxis stepped away from the painting and sat with his friend on the garden bench. He was no sooner seated than two birds flew out of a tree and started to peck at the painted fruit.

"Congratulations," said Parrhasius. "You surely have made the unreal seem real. It will be hard for me to surpass that painting. But I shall try."

More than a month passed before Parrhasius invited Zeuxis to his studio.

"What do you think of it?" he asked, displaying a large painting.

"What do I think of what?" said Zeuxis. "If you will be good enough to draw the curtain aside I will tell you what I think of the picture."

"Ah, my friend," said Parrhasius with a little laugh. "The curtain *is* the picture."

"You have won," said Zeuxis. "I fooled only the birds, but you have fooled me, an artist. Let there be no more rivalry between us, only friendship." They stopped trying to outdo each other; instead they outdid themselves in praise of each other's art.

HERO AND LEANDER

...The Cruel Hellespont

 ETWEEN the Aegean Sea and the Sea of Marmora there lies a long strait separating Europe and Asia. Now called the Dardanelles, in ancient times it was known as the Hellespont. The town of Sestos was on the European side of this narrow body of water and the Asian city of Abydos was on the opposite shore.

Hero was one of the loveliest priestesses in the Temple of Aphrodite in Sestos. It was said that Apollo, the god of poetry and music, courted her for her golden hair and offered to share his heavenly throne with her. But Hero was a dedicated priestess and had sworn never to love a mortal man or even an immortal one. Her beauty surpassed that of all the other priestesses; some claimed that she outshone Aphrodite herself. In the ceremonial processions she seemed to float, a creature in a vision. Scarcely touching the earth, she walked attired in a robe of flowing white, lined in purple silk set off with gilt stars and wide, grass-green sleeves. A myrtle wreath crowned her head, and a flower-embroidered veil fell to her feet. She perfumed the air as she passed by.

It was at an annual festival that she was seen for the first time by Leander, a youth who lived across the Hellespont in Abydos. Struck with her beauty, he stood stone-still. She caught his look and her white face suddenly flamed.

"Who ever loved that loved not at first sight?"

So sang Christopher Marlowe in his poem about lovers, and lovers these two inevitably became. Hero forgot her vow never to love a man and, though she was closely watched, managed to meet Leander every night.

Hero would hang a torch in her tower; Leander would leave his home in Abydos and, guided by her light, swim across the Hellespont, a feat that no man had ever before accomplished. Their meetings were rapturous. She would sing songs of love to him and little prayers to the waters that separated them.

> O waters swift and current strong,
> O waves, divide not lovers long!

The evening before they were to be married, Leander started on his nightly adventure. The sky was heavy with clouds, low thunder rumbled ominously. But Leander was confident. He dived into the Hellespont and cut the waves with steady strokes.

However, when he was halfway across, the waters became rough. A storm mixed the sea with the sky; lightning flashed, and a gale broke towering foam over him. Plunging ahead, Leander kept his eyes on Hero's guiding light until a wave engulfed him. At that moment, the wind blew out her torch.

When he rose he could see nothing. He fought aimlessly against the torrent, but the waves tossed him away from his unseen goal. For a long while he battled in darkness against wind and waves, but he could not overcome the elements.

In the morning the agonized Hero found his body. By a cruel irony it had been thrown up on the shore underneath her tower.

"O waves," she moaned in anguish, "you would not heed my prayers. You have torn my love away from me. But you cannot divide us forever. You cannot keep us apart even for an hour. We will be together now—and always."

And, with a cry, she cast herself into the still churning waters.

THE SEVEN WONDERS OF THE WORLD

...Glories of the Ancients

 HE ancient world was full of marvels, but there were seven wonders that were recorded as the greatest of them all. They were:

The Pyramids of Egypt
The Hanging Gardens of Babylon
The Tomb of Mausolus at Halicarnassus
The Temple of Artemis at Ephesus
The Colossus of Rhodes
The Statue of Zeus at Olympia
The Lighthouse at Alexandria

The first of these wonders is the only one still existing today; the ancients ranked the pyramids above all others in importance. These pyramids had been erected in many parts of Egypt for century after century to serve as royal tombs. In them the bodies of the dead, radiantly clad and often crowned, were surrounded not only with jewels but with furniture, clothes, cosmetics, and even cooking utensils, for it was believed that the deceased would be able to use these things when they awoke in the next world. The largest and perhaps the oldest of these mammoth tombs is the Pyramid of Cheops. It was built five thousand years ago of huge blocks of stone, each block weighing about two tons. More than two million of these blocks went into the construction of Cheops' tomb which covers twelve acres and rises five hundred feet in the Sahara desert near the city of Cairo. It is one of the rare great monuments to an ancient ruler that still stands.

We know about the Hanging Gardens of Babylon only by way of a legend that has outlived the ages. Babylon itself lies under the earth. The excavated ruins and records written on clay bricks reveal how great a city it once was: a city of splendid palaces, huge squares, and broad avenues lined with lordly statuary. Babylon lay on a long, flat plain, and the legend has it that one of its kings married a lovely princess from the mountain country of Media. She missed the hills and upland valleys; she grew so homesick that the king sent for his physicians.

"There is one thing you can do," advised the doctors. "Build something like her own home here. She will feel at home in Babylon only when Babylon looks like Media."

The king could not transform the whole country, but he changed everything around the palace for his beloved queen. He had huge mounds of earth brought in, terraces created, rocks carefully landscaped, and streams diverted to make a lively music. Trees were planted everywhere and blossoming vines draped over stone walls and wooden lattices. Waterfalls ended in chattering brooks, and the brooks ran murmuring into fields full of gay flowers. Looking up at it from below, this landscape seemed suspended in air—like a series of hanging gardens, gardens in which the queen wandered delightedly day after day.

The Tomb of Mausolus in the city of Halicarnassus was both a burial place and a memorial to him designed by his devoted wife. It was one of the most remarkable structures ever built. When Mausolus died, his wife wanted the world to know how great a man he was; therefore the place that was to hold his body had to look equally great. The spot chosen was the side of a solid rock mountain. Workmen chiseled into the rock until there was room for a huge temple wide enough to be faced with thirty-six marble columns. In the interior, the temple had halls with many sculptures and statues, and on the walls were painted scenes from the life of Mausolus. In the very center, in a room carved out of the heart of the rock, the queen placed the body of her husband in a marble coffin. It was a splendid memorial for Mausolus, the kind which ever since then we call a "mausoleum."

The Temple of Artemis was the pride of Ephesus. Artemis (or Diana, as she was called by the Romans) was the moon goddess and was worshipped for her purity. Croesus himself had dedicated thirty-six sculptured columns to her, and the most beautiful girls in the land were her temple priestesses. Her shrine was covered with jewelled ornaments and richly embroidered cloths. Mounted at its center, on a platform of gold, was the statue of the goddess. It was

made of pure ivory and even in the darkness it seemed to shine
with a light of its own.

The Colossus of Rhodes spanned the harbor of the city which had
the same name as the island of Rhodes. Unlike anything ever built,
it was a brass statue more than one hundred feet high, so huge that
a man's arms could not reach around the smallest toe. One foot of
the Colossus rested on the north side of the harbor while the other

was embedded in the south side. Ships passed under it; it served as a beacon as well as a landmark. By day the polished brass reflected the rays of the sun with the power of a thousand mirrors; by night it caught the light of the moon and the stars. It stood for three hundred years and it was, as the name suggests, truly "colossal."

Although the Colossus of Rhodes was the largest statue in the world, the statue of Zeus at Olympia was the most famous and the most revered. Zeus was the greatest of the Olympian gods, and it was fitting that this statue—a majestic, larger-than-life statue—should be in Olympia. It had been carved by Phidias, the greatest artist of ancient Greece, who designed the sculptures for the Parthenon at Athens. It showed Zeus seated on an imperial marble throne, holding his sceptre in one hand and a winged figure in the other. An eagle perched on his shoulder; his brow held concealed thunderbolts; there was a look of lightning in his eyes. His face, hands, arms and feet were carved out of ivory, but ivory that had a faint flush, almost the color of flesh, while the robes which covered the rest of his body were made of beaten gold. The statue was so lifelike it seemed to breathe. It was both godlike and human, natural yet noble, and it stood for centuries.

The Lighthouse (or Pharos) was the pride of Alexandria, the Egyptian city founded by Alexander the Great. The low-lying rocky coast of Alexandria, where the Nile flows into the sea, had caused much damage to shipping. Vessels continually ran aground there or were broken up on the rocks. Near the entrance to the harbor lay a small island, and on it a tower was built to guide ships to safety. The tower was made of beautiful white marble and rose to a height of four hundred feet. It glowed like a pillar of solid sunshine during the day, and the light of twenty torches burning at the top pierced the blackest night. For more than a thousand years it withstood the pounding of fierce waves and the battering of the most violent storms. And when the tower was finally toppled by an earthquake, its pieces were built into a great sea-wall that continued to protect Alexandria and all the ships that harbored there.

ROMULUS AND REMUS

...Sons of the Wolf

 HE Trojan war was over. The proud city had been set on fire and destroyed; most of the defenders of Troy had been slain. One of them, Aeneas, had escaped, carrying his old father on his shoulders out of the burning city. Homeless and heartsick, Aeneas roamed about for many years——the story of his long wanderings is told in the twelve books of the *Aeneid,* an epic poem by Virgil, the great Latin poet. Finally Aeneas settled in Italy, where he made friends, married a king's daughter and founded a colony.

Among his descendants were two brothers, Amulius and Numitor. The older one, Numitor, became king and was a gentle ruler. But his brother, who was crafty and cruel, schemed to get the throne. First by trickery, then by force, Amulius seized power and drove Numitor out of the royal house. To make sure that there would be no heirs to claim their rights to the throne, he put Numitor's son to death. He also wanted to do away with Numitor's daughter, Silvia, but he was afraid that the people would rise against him if he had her killed. Instead he did what he thought a clever thing: he had her appointed a priestess of Vesta, for those who took care of the temple of Vesta were forbidden to marry. And so he assured himself that there would be no children to dispute his kingship.

But Amulius' plan miscarried. Out of the forest came a man. He was stern and mighty of muscle, fierce but fascinating. By his side there walked a wolf, and a woodpecker sat on his shoulder. He saw Silvia, and fell in love with her; she returned his love. She did not know it, but he was a god in disguise, Mars, the god of war. She bore him twin sons, Romulus and Remus.

81

Furious at first, the wily Amulius saw how he could benefit by what had happened. Now he had a good excuse to get rid of the last threat to his throne. He had Silvia thrown into prison and gave orders that her children should be set adrift on the Tiber river. Even in this act, Amulius was crafty. He saw to it that the babes were put into a shallow basket and floated on the roaring Tiber when it was at flood tide.

"If the basket sinks," he said, "let them swim. If they drown, it will not be my fault. The river will be to blame, not me."

The river rose higher than he ever imagined—it rose so high and fast that, before the basket could sink, it was washed ashore. There, on the muddy banks of the Tiber, caught in the reeds, the infants lay, shivering with cold, crying with hunger.

Their cries were heard, not by a human being but by a wandering animal, a she-wolf who had come down to the river to drink. She took pity on the babes, so hairless, so homeless, so hopeless. She gave them milk, carried them to her cave in the woods, and cared for them. As they began to grow, a woodpecker made its home in a nearby tree and, from time to time, brought berries to add to their food. The god of war must have smiled.

So Romulus and Remus grew up a part of the she-wolf's family. They drank her milk, played with the cubs, and shared whatever the mother brought in. They grew bolder, stronger, and more cunning than any of the young wolves in the wood.

One fall hunters came through the forest with dogs and daggers and surrounded the pack. But the wolf-boys were not to be caught. They slipped through the circle and found a cave of their own. There they were discovered by a shepherd who was looking for stray sheep. They snarled and bared their teeth at him, but he seized them by the hair and, though they squirmed and clawed, he brought them to his home.

"Here," he said to his wife, "you always wanted children, and we haven't any. I'm not even sure these two are human but, whatever they may be, here they are. Do you want to keep them, or shall I let them loose?"

She looked at them; she was not frightened. They looked at her; they stopped snarling and rubbed against her.

"I think I want to keep them," she said. "And I think they'll want to stay."

They stayed. For a while they were savage. They pounced upon their food, slept curled up in dark corners, and howled at the full

moon. They were always on the heels of the shepherd's wife, following her wherever she went like a couple of faithful dogs. She was
patient; she showed them how to act like human beings. She tamed
them quietly and taught them with the language of love. Gradually
they lost their wildness. They learned to talk, they learned what to
do with their hands, and how to work things out with their heads.
They grew slim and tall and fair.

As they straightened into young manhood, they became expert shepherds. With an understanding of nature they had learned from the she-wolf, and the authority they had inherited from their royal ancestors, they became the leaders of all the herdsmen in the neighborhood. There were quarrels with other groups of shepherds and fights with gangs of robbers, but the brothers were always victorious. However, one day when they were separated, a large band of marauders took Remus by surprise, captured his flock of sheep, and delivered him to King Amulius for ransom.

When Romulus learned what had happened, he ran to his foster-father.

"I was afraid of something like this," said the old shepherd. "I have been troubled about the two of you for a long time. You have always been strange. You must realize you are not like the others."

"Who are we then?" asked Romulus.

"I'm not sure," said the shepherd, "but I have an idea. When you learned to talk you told me a queer tale. You remembered that you had been cared for by a she-wolf in a shelter near the Tiber. At first this seemed impossible. Then I, too, remembered something. I remembered a rumor that King Amulius had taken the throne away from his brother Numitor, that he had imprisoned or done away with Numitor's daughter, Silvia, had carried off her two sons—twins, according to the story—and cast them into the river. I found you and your twin brother not far from the river and not long after the two infants were supposed to have been thrown into it."

Romulus stared. "You mean——you think Remus and I——?"

"What else is there to think?" replied the shepherd. "I think—at least I guess—you know who you are. Also I think you might have a talk with King Amulius. Or, better still, with your grandfather Numitor. I think it's time for you to do something about it."

The next day Romulus sought out Numitor in his exile. He told him all there was to tell. The ex-monarch looked at the youth a long time before he spoke.

"Yes," he said finally. "There is no question about it. You are of the true blood, the lineage of Aeneas. You are my grandson. And your brother is the prisoner of Amulius, the tyrant who tried to kill you both, who robbed me of my throne. Yet knowing all this, what can you do?"

"I can topple him from his throne," said Romulus. "Right must prevail."

"Perhaps," said Numitor, doubtfully. "But how will you do it? Alone?"

"I can count on many friends. The shepherds will help me."

"Shepherds?" Numitor lifted an eyebrow. "Shepherds for soldiers? And with what weapons?"

"Sticks, stones, clubs, shepherd's crooks—anything we can lay our hands on."

Stout-hearted though Romulus was, he knew his band was no match for the trained troops of Amulius. So at night when the shepherds, together with some of Numitor's staff, were assembled in the dark woods, Romulus devised a strategy. He gave an order that Numitor's men should dash toward the citadel that contained the treasury, rushing with fierce cries and flaming torches. Thinking the citadel was the center of attack, the guards left the king's house to protect the treasury. At that moment, Romulus and his shepherds streamed out of the woods, broke down the gates of Amulius' house, overpowered the remaining soldiers, and rescued Remus. Together the brothers ran through the rooms, smashed the doors of the royal private chambers, and slew the treacherous king. Again the god of war must have smiled—this time with pride.

The fight lasted less than an hour. Peace was restored, Numitor was declared king and, with joyful ceremony, established in his rightful place. Romulus and Remus were acknowledged as the princes, heroic heirs to the throne. Reunited, they swore allegiance to their royal grandfather.

But life at court was not to their liking. It was too tame, too tiresome; there was still a trace of wildness in their blood. They were restless, wanted something greatly, though they did not know what it was. Suddenly they knew. They wanted to found a city, a city of their own. They even knew where it would be. They would build it on the banks of the Tiber, at the very place where they had been left to die.

Gathering their men about them, they set out to find the best place for the first foundation. They waited for a sign. Remus stood on one hill, Romulus on another. To Remus came the first sign: six vultures flying over his head. It was a good omen, for the vulture was a sacred bird, a bird that did not kill but fed only on the dead. It was the bird offered up for important sacrifices.

"We will build here," cried Remus.

But before the six vultures had soared away, another group came out of the heavens and circled above Romulus. This time there were twelve birds.

"The right place is here," shouted Romulus.

Those who stood around Remus claimed that since he had seen

the birds first, the city should be built where he wished, and that Remus should be its first king. Those around Romulus insisted that since he had seen the greater number, this proved he was favored by the gods, and it was Romulus who should rule the city. Both groups argued loud and long; their voices grew angrier. The dispute led to violent conflict, and in the fighting Remus was slain.

Romulus was aghast at what had happened. He tore his clothes in anguish; he bathed the body of Remus with his tears and threatened to kill himself. But the men consoled him, blaming themselves for the tragedy. At last they succeeded in rousing him from despair. They made him realize that they had come here for a purpose, that there was work to be done, a city to be built.

Built it was, a proud city on seven hills, a city whose first king was Romulus. It was named for him: Rome. There Romulus lived and ruled and fought to preserve the city until his death. Before the end, he gathered his people about him and addressed them. "Our city," he said, "shall one day be the greatest city in the world. Let your children teach their children the way of peace and the art of war so that no human strength can ever break the power of the Roman spirit." Then he died.

They buried him in a marble sarcophagus carved with a design showing a basket floating on a river, a she-wolf suckling two little twins, a shepherd and his wife, and, intertwined with all of these, helmets and swords and spears and all the properties of the god of war. On the monument they placed a vulture, the bird of sacrifice, the sacred bird that had shown Romulus the site of his city.

Years passed. The years grew into centuries; centuries piled upon each other. The dust of time sifted over the earth and into men's minds. People began to think of Romulus and Remus as legendary figures, myths rather than men. They doubted that there was any truth at all in their story.

Then one day in 1958, after more than two thousand years had gone by, workmen dug up an ancient site in the Roman Forum. It was thought to be the burial place of Romulus, though further evidence was needed to make certain. They found a marble coffin with traces of carving, but the strangest piece of evidence was a scattering of sacrificial bones upon the tomb. Scientists identified the bones. They were the bones of a bird, the bones of a vulture.

HORATIUS

. . . What He Did at the Bridge

HE story of Horatius is one of the most glorious chapters in the history of Rome. It has been retold and rewritten many times, most stirringly by the English poet and historian, Thomas Macaulay, in his *Lays of Ancient Rome.* It happened this way:
Rome was in great danger. There had been six kings after Romulus. Lucius Tarquinius, known as Tarquin the Tyrant, was the last and the worst. He took away free men's liberty, put honest senators to death, dismissed loyal generals and surrounded himself with a bodyguard of cut-throats. His crimes grew so outrageous that the people finally deposed and banished him. They resolved to have no more kings and, so that no one man would ever have absolute power, they put the government in the hands of two consuls.

But Tarquin had no intention of remaining in exile. He tried various ways to get back his throne, but was always defeated. Finally, he decided to go to the Etruscans for help. Together with his son Sextus, whom the Romans hated as much as they did his father, he went to Clusium, the chief city of Etruria, and pleaded with the King, Lars Porsena.

"There are many reasons why you should join forces with me against Rome," said Tarquin. "For one thing I am an Etruscan by descent. For another thing, I am—or was—a brother-monarch, and it would be a terrible thing for all monarchs if dethronement became popular. Imagine what would happen if people took it in their heads—and worse, into their hands—to rebel against their rulers and adopt the new fashion of toppling kings from their thrones! I know your own people are happy and untroubled but," he added slyly, "there are always trouble-makers. And it is just possible that if their eyes turn to Rome, they might get ideas about having a republic instead of a monarchy."

"I understand you," said Lars Porsena, "and there is something in what you say. Nevertheless, there is nothing to be gained by hurrying into conflict, especially when unprepared. Let us try persuasion before we resort to force."

Lars Porsena had no real quarrel with Rome. At the same time he saw an opportunity of enlarging his kingdom. So he sent ambassadors to Rome. At first they were received courteously, but when they insisted that Tarquin should be restored to the throne, they were scornfully refused.

"Tell your monarch," replied the consuls, "that, once and for all, we are through with kings. The only rulers here are the people. And they rule themselves."

When the answer was brought to Clusium, Lars Porsena summoned Tarquin. "I have made up my mind," he declared. "By the Nine Gods I swear that your house shall suffer no more wrong. Together we will make war on Rome, and you shall have your throne again."

He sent messengers to collect troops not only from the twelve large cities of Etruria but from the smallest villages. They also brought back forces from Lars Porsena's allies: hordes of farmers and workmen as well as soldiers. Young men and men no longer young poured into Clusium, where they were outfitted, armed and trained. Soon there was an army of ninety thousand fighting men— archers, spear-throwers, swordsmen, engineers, experts of the deadly stone-hurling catapult, horsemen and charioteers. Then, when it was time to strike, the signal was given, the war-horns sounded, and the march on Rome began.

The roads were clogged with men and women fleeing from the advancing troops, country folk driving their cattle and carrying their belongings from the farms. For miles around the city families pressed on, mothers with children, old men hobbling on crutches, sick people borne in litters, shepherds with their sheep, flocks of goats, hard-pressed mules, wagons piled with sacks of corn—all crowding toward Rome and the hope of refuge. Villages were looted, sacked, and burned as Lars Porsena's army drew nearer and nearer.

When the news reached Rome, fear filled the streets. Her small army could never hope to oppose Lars Porsena's massive onslaught. Rome's best defense was the River Tiber that could be crossed by only one wooden bridge. Fear increased when the main fort on the Janiculum hill was captured after violent resistance. Now there was nothing left between the enemy and the heart of Rome but that one narrow bridge. When the invaders crossed this, Rome would fall, and the vengeful Tarquin could do what he pleased. The people beseeched the consuls, and the consuls looked desperately to the bridge.

Horatius was the guardian of the bridge at the entrance to the city. He saw the vast army assembled on the opposite bank of the river, and he saw the frightened Romans behind him. There was little time for argument. He spoke directly to the consuls. In the words of Macaulay:

> Then out spake brave Horatius,
> The captain of the gate:
> "To every man upon this earth
> Death cometh soon or late.
> And how can a man die better
> Than facing fearful odds
> For the ashes of his fathers
> And the temples of his gods."

"Give me two men," said Horatius, "and we will hold the bridge a while. It may be for only a short time, but it may be long enough for the bridge to be destroyed. While the three of us hold off the attackers, you must break down the bridge—use axes, crowbars, hatchets, hammers—break it down anyway you can. But hurry! It is our only hope."

Then, turning to the little group of soldiers, he said, "Who will stand with me? Who will risk his life for Rome?"

"I will," cried Lartius. "I will stand at your right side."

"And I," cried Herminius. "I will stand by your left."

The Romans grabbed axes and other tools as Horatius and his companions ran forward to the end of the bridge. Seeing three men opposed to an army of many thousands, a loud laugh went up from Lars Porsena's men. The three companions stood calm and silent. Then, after a pause, Horatius spoke.

"Why do you hesitate?" he taunted Tarquin and the Etruscans. "Are you afraid of three men, men willing to lose their lives for the sake of liberty? Come on then, slaves—slaves who are here at the bidding of your masters to rob us of our freedom, freedom that you do not dare to want for yourselves! Come on!"

For a while the enemy held off. Then, ashamed and angry with themselves because of their shame, they gave a great shout and thrust forward. Three of their chief warriors spurred their horses toward the narrow bridge-head and flung their spears at the three guarding the bridge. But Lartius struck down the first, Herminius slew the second, and Horatius disposed of the third. Three more Etruscans rushed in a group at Horatius, but he did not flinch; he pierced the armor of one, while Lartius and Herminius disarmed and killed the other two. Now the invaders were troubled; their vast army seemed to shrink and hesitate.

"Astur!" a cry went up. "Astur to the front!"

Astur, the Etrurians' champion, strode through the ranks. A giant of a man, he carried a great bronze shield that clanged on his shoulders and brandished a broadsword that no one else could wield. He glanced contemptuously at the flinching Etruscans.

"You let yourself be stopped by a rabble of Romans!" he said scornfully. "Look! the she-wolf's litter stands at bay! It's time for the final kill. Follow me while I clear the way!"

Whirling his great flashing sword with both hands he rushed against Horatius. With his own sword, Horatius deflected the blow.

It missed his head but it gashed his thigh, and at the sight of his blood the Etruscans raised a savage shout. Horatius reeled; he leaned against Herminius for a moment's breath, then sprang at Astur's head. Astur was unprepared for the catlike attack and was thrown off balance. Before Astur could swing his shield into place, Horatius delivered so fierce a swordthrust that the blade crashed through Astur's helmet, smashed his skull, and stood out behind his head as Astur fell. Horatius placed his foot on the mightiest warrior of the Etruscans and mocked the enemy:

"This is the kind of welcome Rome extends to its uninvited guests. Is there anyone else ready to taste our Roman cheer?"

Sullenly the Etruscans drew back, while Horatius strained to hear the sound of axes finishing their work.

What he heard delighted him. The Romans had succeeded in breaking down most of the bridge. It hung tottering above the swirling river. "Come back!" they shouted. "The supports are falling! Come back!"

"Yes, go back," said Horatius to his comrades. "Our work is done."

Lartius and Herminius darted toward safety. Just as they reached the shore where the Romans were standing, the planks cracked, the timbers split, and with a thundering sound the torn beams plunged into the river that boiled and roared and whipped them down the stream.

Horatius was now alone on the enemy bank. Retreat was cut off; there was no way for him to escape. Before the Etruscans could seize and kill him, Lars Porsena spoke.

"You are a brave man, Horatius," he said. "And brave men are not easy to come by these days. I would like to spare your life. Will you join my army and be a conqueror? Or would you rather be a lone man who is about to die?"

Then Horatius spoke. He spoke not to Lars Porsena, but to the river.

"Oh, Father Tiber," said Horatius, "holy river, receive me. Take in sacrifice this soldier and his arms."

He leaped and, as he struck the water, the infuriated Etruscans hurled spear after spear against him. None hit. In spite of his heavy armor, Horatius swam. Friends and foes stared in amazement as the whirling current carried him. They saw him sink and rise and sink again. Once more he rose.

"Curse on him!" cried false Sextus
  "Will not this villain drown!
But for this stay, ere close of day
  We should have sacked the town!"
"Heaven help him!" cried Lars Porsena,
  "And bring him safe to shore;
For such a gallant feat of arms
  Was never seen before."

Lars Porsena's prayer was answered by the Tiber if not by heaven. One great swirl of the current helped Horatius and brought him over to the Roman side, landing him on the bank. The Romans broke into shouts of joy, bursts of clapping, laughing, weeping, cheering. The consuls tried to say something, but they could not be heard. The exultant crowd carried Horatius off on their shoulders.

Countless rewards were offered him. Horatius declined them all. "All I ask is what a man requires to live on," he said. "Let me have only as much land as can be plowed with a yoke of oxen in one day."

They gave him the land. And they gave him more. They gave him a cherished spot in the market place. There they erected a statue in his honor. It was a heroic image of the man who kept a whole army at bay and thought it no more than his simple duty. It stood there for hundreds of years. His story, inscribed on it in gold, has never been forgotten.

With weeping and with laughter
  Still is the story told
How well Horatius kept the bridge
  In the brave days of old.

THE BURNING HAND

...Mucius, True Roman

ORATIUS had saved Rome from being invaded by the Etruscans, but the city was still under siege. Although Lars Porsena, the Etruscan king, remained on the other side of the Tiber, Rome was encircled by his army. No supplies from the outside could reach the inhabitants, and to make matters worse, Porsena stationed ships along the river to cut off the possibility of any food being smuggled into the city. A new calamity faced the Romans: the fear of famine was even greater than the fear of invasion. Men could stand up and fight other men; they could not fight starvation.

Too proud to surrender, too poorly equipped to combat Porsena's powerful army, the Romans were in a critical situation. It was then that a group of young men, headed by Mucius, came to a decision.

"There's only one way to end this siege," said Mucius. "We must rid ourselves of Lars Porsena. He is the head of the great body of forces against us. If a body should happen to lose its head, that body would cease to exist."

"But how can it be done?" they asked. "He is surrounded by armed cohorts. His sentries are on the alert. No soldier could ever get past the guards."

Mucius said only, "When I go, I will not go as a soldier."

The next night, disguised as a farmer carrying a sack of peaches and pears—fruit was a delicacy hard to obtain—Mucius crossed the river. It was a cloudy moonless night; his oars were muffled and no one could hear or see his approach. Mucius hid his small boat in the reeds and at dawn walked down a back road to the enemy camp. The sentries examined his bag. When they were assured no arms were concealed in it, they helped themselves to the fruit, and let him through. What they did not notice was the dagger hidden in his tunic.

Mucius did not dare ask a question; a single word might betray him. He wandered about the camp until he saw a man resplendently dressed and imposing in appearance. Soldiers stood gathered about this person while he gave orders to some and money to others. This must be Lars Porsena, thought Mucius. Grasping the dagger, he sprang at the man and plunged the blade in his breast. The man fell. There was a great outcry and Mucius was held savagely by a dozen hands. The soldiers were about to slay him when they were stopped by a commanding voice.

"Let him go—for a moment at least," said Lars Porsena. "I will deal with him." He turned to Mucius. "You seem to have mistaken the king's steward for the king. It was a costly error. And now, before I have you thrown to the wolves, perhaps you will tell me who you are."

"My name is Mucius. I am a Roman. You are the enemy of my country and I came here to kill you. I have failed. But someone else will succeed."

"I think I won't throw you to the wolves," said Lars Porsena. "And I won't let my soldiers kill you now. That would be too easy and too quick a death. Instead you will perish slowly. I will have you burned alive."

They took Mucius to where a bonfire blazed.

"I would rather die by fire than by famine," he said. "Pain holds no terror for me." Saying this, he plunged his right hand into the flames and held it there until it was burned to the bone.

The men were aghast. They drew back and looked toward the king.

"I have seen many things," said Lars Porsena. "But I have never seen a madder or a more courageous thing than that. What did you hope to gain by it?"

"Nothing," said Mucius, "except to show that where our country is concerned, we Romans have no fear for ourselves. And I will tell you this: if you kill me, another will come to take my place. And if he is killed, there will be another, and then another, until the time comes when you yourself are killed or your army ceases to threaten us."

Lars Porsena smiled a grim smile. "Perhaps that time has come," he said. "If the rest of the Romans are as brave as you, it would be

better to have them as allies than as enemies. Go now and tell your consuls I am ready to talk peace rather than war. Tell them I will no longer fight for Tarquin, that I hope for better allies. Go, and my hopes go with you."

When Mucius returned with the message from Lars Porsena, there was rejoicing throughout Rome. The grateful citizens awarded him a grant of land. They named it after him: the Mucian Meadows. And, in honor of his fearless deed, he was ever after known as Mucius of the Left Hand, Mucius the Fearless.

CORIOLANUS

...The Man Who Loved War

 OWARD the end of the fifth century B. C. Rome was a city unhappily divided into clans and opposing parties. The consuls had become almost as powerful as the kings they had deposed. The patricians, or nobles, were rich and arrogant; the plebeians, or common people, had little except grievances. Most of the army was made up of plebeians, who were poorly paid and, in time of peace, given barely enough money for food. They were forced to borrow from the patricians and, when they could not pay what they owed, the lenders could seize their property and sell them into slavery. If the plebeians broke any of the laws imposed upon them by the consuls, they were beaten brutally or thrown into prison and kept there until they died.

Finally the plebeians rebelled. They refused to be soldiers. They said, since the patricians kept all the spoils of battle and benefited by war, let the patricians do the fighting. To prevent the discontent from growing, the consuls promised to pass new laws in favor of the plebeians, and the men consented to fight. But when the war was over, the consuls forgot their promises and the common people were treated worse than ever.

This time the plebeians did something more drastic: they left Rome and camped on the outskirts of the town. "Let the rich fight their own battles," said their leader.

Learning of this insurrection, the enemies of Rome began to invade Roman territory. The patricians were alarmed; not only were there not enough troops to defend them, there were no farmers to feed them and no servants to wait on them. Messenger after messenger was sent to the rebels, pleading with them, offering concessions to all who would return.

But the plebeians refused to listen. "We have had enough of broken promises," said their leader. "We have lost our trust in you. And you have lost us."

The consuls made one more appeal. They sent their most eloquent persuader, Menenius, a wise and experienced orator. He began by speaking on behalf of the consuls, but, when they interrupted him with angry muttering, he said, "Let me tell you a story."

"What's the story about?" asked the leader, suspiciously. "Is it another story about the noble patricians and how much they love us?"

"No," replied Menenius. "It isn't that kind of story at all. It is a story about a stomach. It begins like this. One day all the different parts of the body refused to do any more work. The arms would not lift the hands, the feet would not take a step.

" 'Why should we run about all day to find food for a stomach that can never get enough?' said the feet.

" 'Yes, why should we toil hour after hour,' said the arms, 'digging in the soil, carrying and cooking, making the hands lift things to fill up that lazy glutton!'

" 'And why,' added the jaws and teeth, 'why must we keep chewing and grinding whenever the stomach calls for food—and it never stops calling! Let the stomach do its own work!'

"Then the stomach replied. 'It's true I have a large appetite, that I am indebted to you for nourishment. But I send this nourishment through the body to all of you. If I were not fed, none of you would be able to do any work. You, arms, would grow weak and flabby; you, feet, could not run; you, jaws and teeth, could not move. All of you would lose your strength and be unable to perform your tasks. The body itself would cease to live.' "

"And what's the meaning of that pretty tale?" asked the leader.

"You know the meaning," answered Menenius. "You are the arms and legs and jaws and teeth; the patricians are the stomach; and Rome is the body. If you don't all work together, you all die—and Rome dies with you."

For a while there was silence. Then the leader spoke.

"Have you nothing to propose?" he said. "Is that the end of your fable?"

"Not quite the end," answered Menenius. "If you will return to Rome, I will propose to the Senate that they appoint special officers to look after your rights—magistrates who will have the power to protect you from unjust acts by patricians or consuls—to guard you against any ill treatment. These officers will be called tribunes, champions of the people. And when any unjust law is proposed or any wrong contemplated, they can prevent it by the power of *veto,* which means 'I forbid it.' "

With that assurance, the plebeians returned to Rome.

For a while, there was peace between the factions. But the patricians continued to look down upon the common people and resented the gains they had won. The patrician who despised them most was a close friend of Menenius. His name was Caius Marcius, but because he was such a great general, and particularly because he had taken the strongly defended town of Corioli, capital city of the Volscians, he had been renamed Coriolanus.

Coriolanus was a man whose good qualities were overbalanced by his heavy faults. He could be generous—he saw to it that his captured enemy, the Volscian general, Tullus Aufidius, was set free —but he could be cold and cruel to his inferiors. He was a loving husband and a devoted father; but he was also hot-headed and haughty, a domineering patrician. Invaluable in war, he was a destructive citizen in times of peace.

After his victory at Corioli his friends urged him to be a candidate for consul. Consuls were not appointed by the patricians, however; they were elected by the people. And Coriolanus scorned to make speeches to the crowds. Disdaining to ask for their votes, he received very few. Rejected by the plebeians, he hated them more than ever.

His hatred found expression a little later. Rome was again suffering from famine—the poor, as usual, suffered most. In this crisis, shiploads of corn began to arrive from Sicily. There was much rejoicing at the prospect of relief. But Coriolanus opposed free distribution.

"If the people want something," he said, "they must learn to give something in exchange."

"What can they offer?" asked Menenius. "They have nothing."

"Let them give up their precious tribunes. They had no right to them in the first place. They got them only by threatening us. Now its our turn to threaten them."

The people were infuriated. Mobs formed in the streets crying "Kill Coriolanus! Kill him!"

The tribunes intervened. They argued with the mob's leaders. "If you want justice to prevail, you must be just and lawful. The law prevents you from killing without trial. Coriolanus should be tried—tried for treason against the state and its people."

A deputation was sent to arrest him. This was too much for the proud soldier. He could stand harm and hurt, but not humiliation.

"Since Rome," he said scornfully to his friend Menenius, "seems to have rejected its protectors, I reject its lawless laws. I have had enough. I am quitting Rome."

"But where will you go?" asked Menenius.

"To those who hate me even more than the Romans," Coriolanus replied bitterly. "I will deliver myself to the enemy."

It was twilight when he entered the chief city of the Volscians. No one recognized him as he went directly to the house of Tullus Aufidius. Aufidius was at dinner with his officers, and Coriolanus sat silent at the fireplace in another room, his face muffled and his head sunk upon his breast. Servants seeing him and, in spite of his clothing, sensing a certain dignity in his bearing, went to Aufidius to inform him about the stranger. When Aufidius came to ask who he was, Coriolanus unmuffled himself and said:

"I am Caius Marcius. I am—or was—also called Coriolanus, for what reason you well know. Because of that name I am your enemy; the name is a witness to the curse I have brought not only upon you but also upon myself. You see me here, once the victor, now a banished Roman, a refugee. But I am not here to ask mercy. If I feared death I would not be sitting at your hearth."

"Then why have you come?" asked Aufidius.

"For revenge—revenge upon those who were my fellow-citizens and who are now my foes. They are your enemies, too. If you have the will to make them pay for the injuries they have done you, tell me and I will join with you. I can fight for you with even more success than when I was against you, because I know the force of the Romans better than you. I know their strength and their weaknesses. But I may misjudge you. If you are not of my mind, if you are too weary to risk another war, do what you will with me, for I am not one to languish in exile."

"What you say touches me deeply," said Aufidius. "Stand up, Caius Marcius, and be of good cheer. I promise you this: you and I will fight side by side. We will have our revenge and enter Rome together."

The Volscian army, led by Coriolanus and Aufidius, overran the countryside, burning and looting villages, and when they came into sight, terror gripped the hearts of the unprepared Romans. They dared not risk a battle in which they were sure to be beaten. The

Senate sent deputies to the opposing camp. Coriolanus scorned
their pleas. Then priests were sent out to reason with him, but he
refused to listen.

"I am deaf to your entreaties," he told the emissaries. "There
will be no truce. This is complete retaliation. You must give up the
lands taken from the Volscians, repeal my banishment, and humble
the plebeians by abolishing the tribunes. Then I will disband this
army."

Rome despaired; the terms were impossible. There was only one
hope left.

The next morning, as the troops were drawn up in battle array, a
long line of women, all dressed in mourning, made their way to the
Volscian encampment. It was a strange procession. Among the
women Coriolanus recognized Volumnia, his mother, Virgilia, his
wife, and his two daughters. He ran to them. Torn between happiness and misery, he wept and threw his arms about them. But they
did not return the embrace.

"Who is this man who stands before us?" said his mother. "Is this
my son, a true-born Roman, or is it a traitor who besieges the walls
of his native country? What can we women say? Should we pray
for your victory and our defeat, or for our victory and your death?
If you and your men march forward, you will have to march over
the body of your own mother, the one who brought you into the
world. Nothing good can come of what you are doing. You will
either triumph over your fellow Romans, or be taken prisoner by
them. Either way my heart will be broken. Can you stop now? Must
you destroy the land of your birth, or the trust of those you are now
leading? What will you do?"

Coriolanus was silent.

"My son," continued his mother, "why do you not answer me?
Do you think it honorable for a man to remember only the wrong
done to him and not remember the good things that have happened,
the honors awarded, the faith of his friends, the love of his family?"

And with these words his mother, his wife, and his children fell,
weeping, on their knees before him.

Shaken with grief, Coriolanus said, "Mother, you do not know
what you have done. You have won a victory for your country and
a mortal defeat for your son."

He gave orders for the invading army to withdraw. The Voscians
sullenly headed back to their own country; Coriolanus went with
them.

There are several conflicting stories about the end of Coriolanus.

One version says that, after his retreat, he could no longer live with himself and took his own life. Another has it that he lived a long time, sorrowing and constantly reproaching himself in exile. Some historians claim that he abandoned his militant career and, under another name, became a hermit. In the favorite version—one with which Shakespeare ends his tragic drama—Coriolanus is killed by Aufidius and the angry Volscians who feel he had misled them.

The Romans never forgot Coriolanus. The place where his mother, his wife, and his daughters had pleaded with him was considered a sacred spot. On it was erected a temple called The Fortune of Women, for it was the women who were fortunate enough to save their city when the men had failed. And it is said that when Coriolanus died all Rome wore mourning for him.

CINCINNATUS

...The Farmer Who Saved His Country

 OME grew into a great city, so great in power and pride that she aroused envy in all the towns and tribes of Italy. Her jealous enemies were everywhere; they waited for her downfall, hoping for the day when she would be humbled. No sooner had Rome signed a truce with one adversary than she was threatened by another.

For more than thirty years after Coriolanus, Rome had been subjected to attacks. The Aequians were the worst of the marauders. They plundered the outlying farms, sacked the villages, and swore to topple Rome's mighty walls. Hoping to avoid another long conflict, the Romans sent messengers to the king of the Aequians setting forth their grievances and suggesting an amicable settlement.

"Tell your complaints to the wind," he told them scornfully. "As for a settlement, we will discuss that after Rome opens her gates to us or, if they are not opened, after we break them down."

Stung by the insult, the Romans declared war and ordered one of their consuls, Lucius Minutius, to lead a force against the Aequians. Unfortunately, Minutius was an inexperienced campaigner; he let himself be drawn through a narrow pass and into an ambush. Trapped, surrounded by the Aequian army, he could hold off the enemy for not more than a day or two. Five horsemen managed to slip through, galloped back to Rome, and warned the Senate of the perilous situation.

In this crisis the Senate turned to Cincinnatus, a famous old soldier who had also served as consul and was now a farmer. He was well over sixty, as wise as he was old, and he took his farming seriously. He had to, for he was anything but wealthy. Though a general, Cincinnatus was not one of those who fattened on the spoils of war. And he had refused to take advantage of his position as consul to accumulate riches. For years he had devoted himself to his well-tilled fields: to the oxen who plowed them, the horses he raised for his own pleasure riding and for the cavalry, to his hunting hounds, his chickens and pigs, his cattle and corn, his olive and fig trees, and his orchards.

He was working in the field when the messengers from Rome reached him. He waited, wondering, for them to speak. Breathlessly, they told him the bad tidings.

"Minutius is outnumbered three to one," they said, after they had explained the situation. "Tomorrow his forces will be annihilated. They need help immediately," they pleaded. "We need you."

Cincinnatus did not hesitate. He took his hand from the plow.

"Bring me my cloak," he called to his wife, "and my sword."

Wiping the earth from his hands, he threw the cloak over his shoulders and fastened the sword about his waist. He left the plow where it was, the oxen still standing in the furrow.

Hurrying to Rome, he called all citizens to arms and organized them. Those fit for military service would appear at noon in the Campus Martius to be equipped for battle; those too old or too weak to bear arms would prepare the provisions. Shops were closed, prayers offered, and martial law proclaimed as the hastily assembled men and boys marched out of the city.

They marched until they neared the narrow pass where Minutius and his men were trapped. Cincinnatus stopped in the rear of the Aequians. He had his men cut down boughs and saplings and carrying these, hidden behind the screen of leaves, they advanced stealthily. Then with a shout they sprang upon the Aequians. Before the enemy knew what had befallen them, they were attacked on one side by the army of Cincinnatus and, on the other, by Minitius' men. Held at bay, encircled, they were cut to pieces. To save the rest of his force from being slaughtered the Aequian king quickly surrendered.

Cincinnatus granted him and his men their lives, but only on one condition: the Aequian army must pass "under the yoke." Two spears were thrust upright into the ground, a third tied across the tops. This was the "yoke," and under it, as a token of submission, the disarmed Aequian army walked with bowed heads while the Roman army, drawn up in two long lines on either side, mocked the beaten enemy. So great was this disgrace that it became a by-

word: the Latin phrase *sub* (under) *jugum* (a yoke) became *subjugate,* meaning to compel subservience, to subdue and conquer.

The grateful Romans wanted to give Cincinnatus great powers as well as spoils of war. He refused.

"All the power I need is the power of my hands upon the plow," he said. "As for spoils, we are fortunate that our troops were not themselves the spoils of the Aequians. Let us be done with greed and violence. Let us work, not fight, for what we need."

Nevertheless, the people clamored for Cincinnatus to be their leader; they urged him to set aside the consuls and rule as king or, if he did not want to be king, to become their dictator.

For sixteen days Cincinnatus remained in Rome as the head of government. Then he left. He realized he was not made to be a ruler. He did not want to be his country's dictator; he was content to be its deliverer.

Cincinnatus went back to the farm.

THE CAPITOLINE GEESE

...*How the Birds Saved Rome*

NCE more Rome was besieged. This time a horde of barbarians had managed to occupy the lower part of the town and surround the fortress which stood on the top of the Capitoline, highest of Rome's seven hills. From the fortress walls the Romans hurled down rocks, spears, and arrows at the invading Gauls who were unable to storm the steep slope, but hoped to starve the defenders into surrendering. To taunt Bran, the invading commander, the Roman garrison (though actually suffering from hunger) threw loaves of bread into the enemy camp.

Bran could not understand this; it puzzled and irritated him. "If the Romans are so well supplied with food that they can use bread for stones, they can't be starving," Bran said to himself. "This is going to take a long time, unless we find a better way to make them come to terms."

The next night Bran found what seemed a better way. One of his sentries spied a Roman stealthily climbing down the rocky incline from the Capitoline hill. The Roman was creeping along a narrow cleft on a secret mission, seeking help from some troops who were encamped beyond the Gauls. When Bran was informed of this, he asked the sentry to point out the way the Roman had descended. Then, making sure of the path up the cliff, the commander of the Gauls determined to assault the heart of the city.

In the darkest hour of the night, one armed soldier after another groped his way up the sharp incline. Used to mountain passes, the Gauls had little trouble climbing almost to the top. The place was dark. Having noticed no activity in weeks on the part of the Gauls, the Romans thought themselves safe and were asleep. The troops who had been away from Rome when Bran encircled the city, were waiting tensely in neighboring towns. All that remained to guard the place were small detachments of swordsmen and bowmen and about eighty old senators and priests.

The invaders crawled upward in silence until one of the Gauls scraped his armor against a stone. This woke a flock of geese, the birds sacred to Juno; they had been spared even when the Romans were famished. There was a sudden babble, then a noise of scurrying and hissing. The night became an explosion of furious cackling and whirring of heavy wings.

The noise woke one of the guards, Marcus Manlius, who sat up to see what had aroused the geese to such wild clamor. What he saw was a barbarian climbing over the wall. In a moment Manlius was on his feet. He rushed to the wall just in time to strike the invader over the head and send him hurtling down. In falling, the Gaul threw the one below him off balance, and the climb became a welter of scrambling soldiers trying to get out of the way of what seemed an avalanche.

The cries and clatter brought out the rest of the garrison. There was a blare of trumpets, and Bran found himself attacked on two fronts: the swordsmen and bowmen from the Capitol, and the encamped soldiers who had been waiting for some such signal and now charged into the enemy's ranks.

Bran's army was broken; the retreat turned into a rout. Rome was not only rescued but restored. Manlius was rewarded with the present of a house and a new name, Manlius Capitolinus, in honor of the Capitol he had defended.

The real heroes, however, were the geese. They were carried lovingly, triumphantly, about the city. When they died, surfeited with petting and rich food, they were not forgotten. Every year on the anniversary of the victory, a goose, lying on a bed of softest down and housed in a cage of gold, was borne through the streets of Rome. And in the temple of Juno was placed a golden statue of a goose. It faced the wall of the Capitol, and it is said that once a year, and always at the same hour, the statue would open its beak and give a loud warning cry.

THE PYRRHIC VICTORY

... The Price of Winning

YRRHUS was neither a Roman nor a friend to Rome. On the contrary, he was one of her most envious rivals. A Greek, king of Epirus, Pyrrhus had been favored by the gods; if it had not been for them, his life would have ended almost before it began.

His father had been killed in battle, whereupon his uncle seized the throne and saw to it that all the dead king's relatives were murdered. Pyrrhus was still a baby but, as heir to the throne, he too was marked for murder. The fates intervened, however, and a few faithful servants bundled him up and smuggled him out of the palace. They were followed and, though they managed to evade their pursuers, they were soon stopped by a mountain stream that the rains had flooded and turned into a raging river. It was impossible to wade across. The servants saw some woodcutters working on the other side and shouted to them for help. But the roaring river drowned their cries. Their pursuers were almost upon them. Then one of men pulled some loose bark from a tree, scrawled a message on it telling who the baby was, tied it to a stone and hurled it to the other side. When the workers read the note, they rapidly chopped down some young trees, made a raft, and brought the child across.

The servants took the baby to Glaucias, king of Illyria, and it was here that, thanks to the gods, Pyrrhus' life was spared again. King Glaucias feared to keep the child because he was an ally of the Macedonian ruler who had been at war with Pyrrhus' father. Glaucias was about to turn the infant over to the Macedonians when the baby tottered to an altar in the throne room and held on to it with both hands. At that moment the sun, which had been hidden behind a cloud, came out and shone on the child's face.

Glaucias stared for a moment; then he spoke.

"The child has appealed to the gods," he said, "and they have answered. They have spoken for him. He is in their hands—and ours. Here," he said to his wife, "care for him and keep him until the gods decide what he is to do."

The gods spoke again when Pyrrhus. was twelve. He and King Glaucias were out in the fields watching a group of the king's soldiers practicing spear-throwing. They flung pointed spears at targets thirty, forty, and even fifty feet away. Suddenly one of the men lost his footing as he hurled his spear. It went wide of the mark and flew directly at Pyrrhus. Pyrrhus did not step aside; he calmly raised his hand and caught the weapon just before it struck his head.

"The gods are still on your side," said Glaucias to Pyrrhus. "This, certainly, is a powerful sign. It is time for you now to do what you are meant to do and I will help you. We will go to your homeland together."

Aided by Glaucias, Pyrrhus recovered the throne from his uncle and, at that early age, dedicated himself to war. As he grew into manhood he thought only about soldiering, about cohorts and strategies.

In one of his rare moments of quiet he was listening to two flute players. One of them played a lively air, the other a slow lovely melody. "Your Majesty, which did you like best?" asked one of the musicians, "the gay tune or the sad one?"

"Neither," said Pyrrhus. "The sound I like best is the sound of clashing swords and the song of the arrow as it leaves the bow."

Pyrrhus was fond of his daughters, but his sons delighted him most. He watched them with a combination of pride and worry. "Which boy have you picked to succeed you?" asked Cineas, his chief adviser.

"I can't tell yet," replied Pyrrhus. "I will wait to see which one handles his sword better and which throws his spear further."

A quick-tempered man, he was also a sensible one. When Cineas called his attention to a man who was spreading evil gossip about him in Epirus, Pyrrhus flared up for a moment. Then he said, "If I have him killed or banished, everyone will believe I did it because he told the truth. Let him alone. Let him speak ill of me here. If we drive him away, he will speak ill of me everywhere."

Unable to enjoy a peaceful life, Pyrrhus spent most of the time on battlefields where he felt at home. Sometimes he lost a battle, but he seldom failed to win a campaign. As soon as he finished one campaign, he engaged on another and a larger one. Always in action, he added more and more territories to his own. As he grew older he grew even more ambitious, more greedy for further conquests. He wanted not only to extend his kingdom but, like Alexander the Great, to rule the world.

He was forty when one of his allies, the Greek colony of Tarentum, was threatened by Rome. Pyrrhus rejoiced. This was what he had been waiting for: an opportunity to pit his strength against the proud imperial city.

Cineas advised against the venture.

"The Romans," he said, "are a great and warlike people. Even supposing the gods continue to favor you, what benefit will you derive from a victory over the Romans? What will you do after that?"

"The answer to your question is simple," replied Pyrrhus. "Once I have subdued Rome I will conquer the rest of Italy."

Cineas paused a moment. Then he resumed, "And after you have all the wealth and power of Italy in your hands, what will you do then?"

"Then," said Pyrrhus, "I will go on to Sicily. It is rich, close to Italy, and easily taken."

"And after Sicily," said Cineas, stubbornly pursuing his questioning, "what then?"

"Then," said Pyrrhus, "if the gods please, I will go into Africa, and so to Carthage."

"And after that?" asked Cineas.

"Oh, after that, my good Cineas," said Pyrrhus, laughing, "Then we can rest, have feasts, make merry, and take our ease."

"In that case," said the wily Cineas, "what is there to prevent us from feasting and making merry now? Why must we wait to enjoy ourselves? Why not rest now before so many towns have been destroyed, so many lives lost?"

Pyrrhus turned away. He was offended that Cineas had tricked him, the more so since he knew that Cineas was right. But Pyrrhus' mind was set; he could not halt his ambitious drive. He went to Tarentum.

What he saw there disappointed and angered him. His allies in Tarentum were rich, indolent, and pleasure-loving. They were eager to add Rome's riches to their own—if someone else did the fighting. They talked mightily of war, but spent their time strolling in the parks, idling at the baths and at luxurious banquets. Pyrrhus at once put a stop to that. He shut up the parks and places of entertainment, forbade all games, fun and feasting. He compelled the men to abandon their sports for the tougher disciplines of war. Drilling them morning and night, he sent them on long forced marches and hardened their spirits as well as their bodies.

Finally he was satisfied. He surveyed his army. Including reinforcements from his allies, he now had twenty thousand horsemen, three hundred thousand foot-soldiers, countless special marksmen, and twenty elephants from India, trained for combat. Part of this array he held in reserve, and part he shipped on galleys and flat-bottom boats to the western coast of Italy.

On the way Pyrrhus suffered a devastating and almost fatal setback. An out-of-season tempest blew the ships about; some were smashed against the rocky shore, others lost in the howling sea. Doggedly, he reassembled the remaining forces and prepared to attack.

First, however, he sent a herald to the Romans telling them that he would withdraw his troops if they were willing to settle matters amicably. He suggested arbitration and nominated himself as arbitrator. Levinius, a Roman consul, replied swiftly.

"By what right do you come so threateningly?" asked Levinius. "For that matter, by what right are you in Italy at all? We do not consent to your being here, least of all as a judge. We do not want you as a friend, and we do not fear you as an enemy."

Pyrrhus waited no longer. As both armies were drawn up along the banks of a river, he ordered his men to ford the stream and charge. The fighting was furious. Pyrrhus rode recklessly into the fiercest part of the fray, spurring his horse ahead into the front lines. His ornate armor and golden helmet distinguished him, an easy target for the enemy. One of his officers warned him to be more careful of his person.

"I'm not afraid," said Pyrrhus. "Let come what will from the Romans or any others. No man can escape his destiny."

One of his best generals, wearing Pyrrhus' armor, was mistaken for the king and slain. The news spread, bringing terror to the troops. But Pyrrhus appeared among them bare-headed, waving to them and showing that he was safe. The foot soldiers cheered, the cavalry charged, and the enemy lines wavered. The Romans were not prepared for the final blow, a mass assault by the elephants. They had seen one or two of these great beasts in the circus, but they had never met a whole company of such monsters with their gigantic crushing feet, bellowing, brandishing their pointed tusks, and driving everything before them.

It turned out to be another triumph for Pyrrhus. But he had lost more than half his foot-soldiers and most of his best horsemen. When his officers congratulated him on the victory, Pyrrhus smiled grimly. "One more such victory," he said, "and we are ruined." The phrase was not forgotten. After that day every hard-won triumph achieved at too great cost was known as "a Pyrrhic victory."

But Rome was not to be conquered. Nor would the Romans accept Pyrrhus' terms of peace.

"Rome is like the Hydra, the nine-headed snake," said Cineas. "Strike off one of its heads and it is replaced by two others."

Pyrrhus sent Cineas to deal with the Romans, to threaten and, if necessary, to bribe them. Nothing was accomplished, and Pyrrhus withdrew to Tarentum for the winter.

Rome sent envoys there to confer with him about the ransom of prisoners held by Pyrrhus. The chief Roman ambassador was Fabricius; this was the man Cineas had tried unsuccessfully to bribe while in Rome. He warned Pyrrhus that Fabricius was an honest man, poor in property but rich in integrity. Pyrrhus smiled.

"No man can resist a big offer if he is poor," he said. "Let us see how long he will stand out against the good things of this world."

Pyrrhus then proceeded to make much of Fabricius. He entertained him lavishly, drank toasts to him, and offered him gifts—not for anything Fabricius might do in return, said Pyrrhus, only as a pledge of goodwill and friendship. When Fabricius thanked him for his hospitality, Pyrrhus insisted that his guest take a hamper full of gold and silver as a memento of his visit.

Fabricius shook his head. "It is useless," he said. "If I am honest, I cannot accept a bribe. If I am dishonest, I cannot be trusted and am therefore not worth bribing. Instead of taking something I will *tell* you something. Your favorite physician has written to me offering, for a certain payment, to put poison in your food. This would, of course, end all conflict between you and Rome. But that is not my way of settling things. It seems, Pyrrhus, that you have made a poor choice of both your friends and your enemies."

Pyrrhus accepted the rebuke and the warning handsomely. Grateful for Fabricius' noble magnanimity, he released all the prisoners without ransom. The physician, of course, was disposed of quickly.

The rest of Pyrrhus' life was occupied with other wars—with Sicily, with Macedonia, with Sparta, and again with Rome. He won and lost and won again. He did not live, however, to conquer the world. His end was inglorious and ironic. During some street fighting he was killed, not by some famous adversary or even a common soldier, but by a woman, a very old woman. A piece of tile thrown by her from a rooftop struck Pyrrhus on the head. He died instantly.

REGULUS

...The Fatal Promise

ARTHAGE was Rome's most dangerous enemy, her rival for control of the Mediterranean, which the Romans liked to call "Our Sea." They were a match for each other. If Rome had the more formidable land forces, Carthage had by far the greater sea power. Carthage had been founded by the Phoenicians, a Punic race of seafaring traders, and the Carthaginians had inherited their ship-building and sea-going skills.

Originally Rome was little concerned about Carthage because Carthage seemed too far away in Africa to be a serious threat. However, as the Carthaginians built up trade all along the Mediterranean shores of Europe and accumulated colonies of their own, the Romans grew worried. When Carthage invaded the island of Sicily, which lay so close to the southern point of Italy, Rome became alarmed. It was an easy crossing, too easy. The possession of Sicily by Carthage could not be tolerated. To recapture the island required not only a considerably army, which Rome could quickly raise, but a fleet mighty enough to challenge the Carthaginian navy. This Rome did not have.

It was not long before Rome engaged upon a frantic program of ship building—all warships. She had much to learn, for her boats had always been small and slow—mainly merchant vessels—with single decks and no striking power. Taking as a model the solidly built and extremely fast Carthaginian ships that had three and sometimes five decks, with three to five tiers of rowers on each side, Rome accumulated an imposing fleet. The Carthaginian sailors had learned many tricks for crippling their opponents. One of them was to have a ship row swiftly toward an enemy ship and then, suddenly thrust along the side of the vessel, breaking all the oars on that side. This left the enemy ship helpless and easy to capture, even if it did not overturn.

The Romans improved upon this device. To the prow of their ships they attached a wide board that was actually a gangplank that could be swung about by means of pulleys. The underside of the board had a concealed iron spike at the end, whose point could be dropped with great force. When the Roman ship drew near its adversary, the board would be dropped, the spike jammed into the enemy's deck, and, using the plank as a kind of bridge, the soldiers would swarm aboard.

The Romans waited until they had one hundred vessels. Then one of the consuls was put in command, a note of defiance was sent to Sicily, and the First Punic War, the first of a long series, began. The early victories went to the Carthaginians. The inexperienced Roman sailors were outwitted; their ships were often blockaded and the crews demoralized. After a while, the fortunes of war shifted. Sometimes they veered in favor of the Romans, sometimes of the Carthaginians. The struggle dragged on.

In the ninth year of the war Regulus was made commander of the Roman sea and land forces. A brave general, hero of many battles, he was a man of unusual character. He never made a promise that he could not keep, and he had never broken his word. Since the Carthaginians were better at naval battles, he decided to attack them on land in their own country. He landed in North Africa and proceeded to march toward the capital city. His troops, however, were ambushed, and in the battle that followed, the Romans were disastrously beaten. Regulus was taken prisoner.

The Carthaginians could rejoice at this victory, but on other fronts they had been losing ground to the Romans. It was decided that emissaries should be sent to Rome to negotiate certain peace terms. They called in Regulus, to whom they made no mention of Roman successes. On the contrary, they told him that things were going badly in Italy. He was not deceived, but he said nothing.

"We are willing to let you go to Rome with our emissaries," they said. "But you go on one condition. If Rome accepts our proposals, you are free to remain there. But if our terms are rejected, you must swear to return here as our prisoner."

"I accept the condition. But I do not need to swear," replied Regulus. "You have my word. That is enough."

Knowing his reputation, they let him go. When Regulus arrived in Rome he was greeted by cheering crowds who escorted him to the Senate. But he shrugged them off.

"I am no returning hero," he said. "I am not even a Roman soldier; I come as a Carthaginian prisoner. I have been sent to give a report. After that we will see."

The emissaries from Carthage made their proposals. Their terms, they said, were hard but fair, for the Romans must realize that they were sure to be defeated in the end. They looked to Regulus for confirmation.

Then Regulus spoke. "Do not listen to them," he said. "Do not accept their terms. They are humiliating and would only encourage the other enemies of Rome. It is true that Carthage is strong, but it is not true that Carthage is invincible. Do not surrender, but pursue the war to the end. Rome was not built to be destroyed by African marauders. I have given my word to return to Carthage, but I did not promise to tell a lie. I have said what I know is the truth. Now send me back."

The senators would not hear of it. They were even willing to accept the terms rather than have Regulus returned to Carthage and what they knew would be his death. "Let us defy them," they argued. "At least let us send another man in your place." But Regulus could not be dissuaded.

"I have given my word," he said. "I cannot break it. I must return."

The emissaries were speechless with anger; they turned their backs upon him. Regulus was kept in chains until he reached Carthage. The chains were still on his hands when, because the Romans had rejected their terms, the Carthaginians struck off his head.

HANNIBAL

... *The Unfulfilled Oath*

 HE First Punic War ended when the Carthaginians were finally forced out of Sicily and had to admit defeat. The truce was followed by twenty years of uneasy peace. During that time Rome looked across the Mediterranean, apprehensively watching Carthage for signs of rebellion, while Carthage, smoldering with resentment, eyed Rome with hatred.

No one hated Rome as much as Hamilcar, Carthage's ablest general. Waiting for a time when Carthage would be avenged and her prestige restored, he sullenly taught himself patience and lived on bitterness. In the meanwhile, he led expeditions to other parts of northern Africa, took his troops across the narrow Straits of Gibraltar, and colonized more than half of Spain. He brought his small, dark-skinned son, Hannibal, with him wherever he went, always reminding him to detest anything Roman.

When the boy was nine years old, he saw Hamilcar offer a sacrifice for victory. Hannibal stood near the altar, watching and wondering. His father then turned to his son.

"I am going on a long and hard expedition. I should send you back to Carthage," said Hamilcar, "but I am not certain whether you will be happier safe at home or in danger here with me. What do you say?"

"Let me go with you," answered Hannibal quickly. "You know I am not afraid."

"I know. But I wanted you to say it. I want you to know all the trials and terrors of war and what they may lead to. Here," he said, taking Hannibal's right arm. "Place your hand upon the sacrifice and take this solemn oath. Repeat these words after me: 'I swear to be the enemy of all Romans. I swear to keep my hate alive. I swear never to rest until Rome has been put down and destroyed.' It is a large oath for a little boy, perhaps too large. Do you think you can remember it?"

When Hannibal looked at his father, it was not with the look of a nine-year-old.

" 'I swear to be the enemy of all Romans,' repeated Hannibal. 'I swear to keep my hate alive. I swear never to rest until Rome has been put down and destroyed.' I will not forget."

Hannibal never forgot. He was eighteen when his father was killed fighting in Spain. After that he shared command of the troops with Hasdrubal, his brother-in-law, and when Hasdrubal was slain, he became the chief. He was twenty-six when he besieged the Spanish city of Saguntum.

Saguntum was under the protection of Rome and, in answer to an appeal, Rome sent an envoy cautioning Hannibal to respect the protectorate and warning him against attacking the city. Rome, he added, would consider it a declaration of war if Hannibal should ever cross the Ebro River. Hannibal ignored the warning.

"Say to your consuls," he told the envoy, "that I shall take Saguntum. Then tell them that it is only a beginning. I shall go through Spain, cross over the mountains, and march on Rome. And I will not be stopped."

The Romans were angry but not too alarmed. They told themselves that Hannibal's threat was mere boasting, that his army could never cross the impassable barrier of the Alps, that the braggart would be stopped if he ever advanced too far.

For eight months Hannibal faced Saguntum. It was a long and seemingly endless siege. His troops were poorly fed; they ran out of provisions after the country around them had been stripped; they longed for the good things of Carthage. Hannibal worked with his men, helped with the meanest labors, dug trenches with his own hands. Finally Saguntum fell. The town was looted, and the soldiers refreshed themselves for a few weeks. Then Hannibal reorganized his men, moved north, and the Second Punic War began.

He started with some thirty thousand foot soldiers and less than six thousand horsemen. But as he went he gathered recruits from Carthage's many provinces, from Gaul, Rome's northern enemy, and captives from Spanish towns.

By the time Hannibal crossed the Ebro his was a mighty army, a formidable mixture of black men and brown, trained native troops, eager youths from Carthage, sullen Spaniards, half-naked Gauls. There were now ninety thousand infantry, twelve thousand cavalry, long trains of wagons with horses and pack mules, and forty of the largest elephants to be found in Africa. All along the way there were battles but nothing could stop the advance of the great army.

The elephants presented a special problem. They were used to wading small streams, but they balked at the rapid river currents. Hannibal solved the dilemma. He had rafts constructed and fastened to the bank so that they projected across the water. Then the floats were thickly covered with mud so that they seemed a continuation of the road. Led by trained female elephants, the huge but docile beasts went across. A few became panic-stricken and plunged into the stream, but they managed to swim ashore. The columns went on doggedly.

As the army advanced, difficulties increased. Rome sent troops to harass the expedition; local tribes attacked from the rear. Hannibal shook them all off. His columns, twenty miles long, pushed their way through dangerous passes, toiled along roads that shrunk to thin and treacherous paths, climbed over hills that hid concealed raiders who hurled rocks and boulders at them. Nothing could deter Hannibal, and nothing threatened to stop him until he came to the Alps.

The ascent was terrifying; the descent was worse. As the army climbed, snow fell. It snowed continually. The roads were ice and the paths narrowed and wound along the side of cliffs that had a sheer drop of a thousand feet. Men and beasts slipped on the icy surface or were buried in snowdrifts; hundreds were lost in the deep gullies and precipices. The elephants suffered most. There was no green fodder, no trees for browsing, no place to lie down. Accustomed to the warm sands of Africa, they could barely withstand the freezing cold; they trumpeted in fear and bellowed with pain. Many of them perished.

It took nine days of slow torture to get to the top. By the time the summit was reached, Hannibal had lost half his forces. The remainder dragged themselves painfully. The beasts had been driven almost beyond their endurance; the men were downcast and desperate. Hannibal refused to be disheartened.

"We have done what no army has ever done before," he told his troops. "We have surmounted the impossible barrier. We will make

a two-day pause here, then go on to reap the reward for what we have endured. Look!" he pointed down to the distant valley. "There, beyond the Alps lies Italy. There lies Rome!"

Five months had passed since Hannibal had started from his base in Spain. A few days after descending from the Alps into fertile fields he encountered the spearhead of the Roman armies. This was at Trebbia. Here the Romans were led by a skilled troop of cavalry, which proved to be their undoing. The horses, frightened not only by the sight of the elephants but by the strange smell of these monsters, screamed, threw their riders, and bolted wildly through the lines. The whole front was thrown into disorder, and the Romans lost the first combat.

The elephants served Hannibal well on another occasion. Fabius, the Roman general, realizing he could not overthrow Hannibal in a pitched battle, devised a strategy of slowing down his advance,

cutting off his reinforcements, and hemming him in. He succeeded in bottling up a great part of Hannibal's army in a ravine. There he intended to hold them until they starved or surrendered. But Hannibal was equal to the emergency.

One night, as soon as it grew dark, he sent a dozen of the largest elephants against the enemy. The beasts' heads were painted to make them look frightful; bells clanged along their sides; their tusks were sharpened; on their backs were fastened small wooden towers from which men flung down barbed javelins. The elephants charged, roaring with rage. When a path had been cleared, Hannibal completed his strategy. He had several hundred oxen with flaming torches tied to their horns, driven down the pass. Maddened by the sparks that dropped on their hides, screaming with pain as the torches burned the roots of their horns, they stampeded, swirling through the Roman troops, setting fire to the camp. At the height of the confusion Hannibal's army came out, struck rapidly, driving the Romans from their position, and surged triumphantly out of the ravine.

Hannibal defeated the Romans again at Lake Trasimenus, and even more disastrously at Cannae. There was little resistance as he made his way south. Then, within a few miles of the very gates of Rome, Hannibal stopped. Why? Perhaps he had allowed his weary army to rest too long and too well; feasting and enjoying the pleasures of their winter quarters at Capua, the Carthaginians had grown flabby and lost their fighting spirit. Rome had been greatly strengthened by help from her allies and perhaps Hannibal, with his now inferior force, realized he would have to wait until later for a mass attack and final victory. Still another reason given for the failure to complete his triumph was Carthage's inability to send the reinforcements needed for a crushing blow. In any case, Hannibal postponed the crucial moment, campaigned in other parts of Italy, and fought a delaying set of encounters throughout the country.

Five years later, when the Roman general Scipio changed the situation by taking the offensive in Africa, Hannibal abandoned Italy to save Carthage. While there he was treacherously betrayed and, rather than be put in chains and paraded as a captive through the streets of Rome, he killed himself.

This intrepid military genius, the most formidable opponent Rome ever met, and the patriot who was one of the greatest generals of all time, had been unable to keep his oath. He had not taken and destroyed Rome.

CORNELIA

... The Real Jewels

HEN she was young, Cornelia was known as the daughter of Scipio Africanus, the Roman general who conquered the Carthaginians. When she married, she was known as the wife of Sempronius Gracchus, a famous consul who brought peace to Spain. When she grew old, people spoke of her as the mother of the two great statesmen, Caius and Tiberius Gracchus. And it was as the mother of these two that she is remembered.

While her husband lived, Cornelia was wealthy. After his death she had to sell most of the property, dispose of her valuables, and learn to live simply. She continued to be honored as a noble lady and cherished by her many friends.

One day, while Cornelia was sitting in the garden with her two boys, a particularly rich Roman matron visited her. Fond of display, she had brought her jewel case with her. Her arms glittered with bracelets, a diamond brooch gleamed on her shoulder, and strands of pearls were twined in her hair—in striking contrast to Cornelia who wore no ornament of any kind.

"You were always fond of lovely things, Cornelia," she said. "Would you like to look at some of my treasures?"—and from her jewel case she took necklaces of woven gold, a tiara of Persian turquoise, pins of carved coral and jade, rings set with royal amethysts, with blood-red rubies, sea-green emeralds, and sky-blue sapphires.

Then, putting the last of her gems back into the case, she said in a pitying voice, "Is it really true, Cornelia, that you have lost all your wealth?"

Cornelia smiled. "Not quite all," she said.

"But your jewels?" she said, looking pointedly at Cornelia's un-adorned neck and arms. "Where are they?"

"Here," said Cornelia proudly, putting her arms about her young sons. "These are my jewels."

The two boys, Tiberius and Caius Gracchus, grew up to be true ornaments of the state. As tribunes they were reformers, opposing the ruling rich and defending the poor. At one time the patricians bribed colleagues to undermine their influence, and the fickle mob turned against them. But later the people repented of their folly and erected statues to them as great statesmen. Particular honor was paid to Cornelia, and on her tomb the Romans inscribed this sentence: "Cornelia, Mother of the Gracchi."

CROSSING THE RUBICON

...Caesar's Great Decision

ULIUS Caesar was the idol of Rome. Although he was a patrician, he was always mindful of the plebeians and they, in turn, were devoted to him. He planned great festivals for the people and paid the costs out of his own purse; he divided his spoils of war with them, made laws in their favor, and saw to it that they never went hungry. His soldiers worshipped him. He knew them all by name, ate the same food they did, slept as they did upon a hard camp bed, and often marched along on foot with them. One of the world's greatest commanders, he was also a witty and good companion who loved listening to songs and telling stories. Once, when he was held for ransom by pirates, he told jokes, played games, and recited poetry to his captors who were so delighted that they treated him like a guest instead of a prisoner. It was part of the joke that, after he was ransomed, he immediately captured his captors.

Everyone praised him; Rome resounded with the wonder of his accomplishments. He had taken Gaul, which included France, Belgium and Switzerland, and had occupied Britain. In eight years he had fought countless battles, subjugated three hundred tribes, taken eight hundred cities, and had brought back a million prisoners to work for Rome.

There seemed to be no end to what Caesar could do. He had always been ambitious. Even as a very young man he had made up his mind to reach the top—then go beyond it. During an early campaign, while Caesar was passing through a little town in Spain, the mayor apologized for the smallness of the place.

"Size is unimportant," Caesar assured him. "What is important is leadership. I would rather be the first man in a village than second man in Rome."

It was his determination to be first man in Rome that alarmed those in power, particularly the consul Pompey. After Caesar had conquered Gaul and had offered himself as a candidate for consul, Pompey sent word that he could come to Rome as a private citizen, but not accompanied by his troops. Caesar replied that he would disband his army if Pompey would do the same. This infuriated Pompey; he denounced Caesar and made the Senate agree to brand him a public enemy if he came with his cohorts. Caesar hesitated. He addressed his legions.

"Men, you have been loyal soldiers, and you know me as a loyal son of Rome. What am I to do now? Shall I send you back to your homes? Or shall we make a just claim, the claim that our victories should be acknowledged? Shall we go to Rome—together?"

The cheers told him what he knew would be the answer. The troops started toward Rome, flags flying, led by the standard-bearers carrying stout poles topped with the figure of a lordly eagle, the symbol of triumph. When they came to the town of Ravenna, they stopped.

Once again Caesar hesitated. A few miles south of Ravenna flowed a small stream, the Rubicon, that formed the boundary between Cisalpine Gaul and Italy. As the conqueror and commander of Gaul, Caesar was within his rights there; it was his province. However, the moment he crossed the stream he would be in Roman territory and would be defying not only Pompey but the Senate. By a strict interpretation of the law he would be committing treason.

"We could draw back," he thought to himself. "Once across the river, it will be too late. The choice is between safety and possible civil war. I must decide, and I must decide now."

At that moment a shepherd came down the road, playing on a reed pipe. Some of the Caesar's men followed him, laughing. Imitating them, the shepherd strutted like a soldier, seized a trumpet and blew on it as he walked across the bridge.

Caesar saw and heard. "It is an omen," he said. "The die is cast. We cross the Rubicon. On to Rome!"

Caesar's character lives in that daring phrase. Although it was uttered two thousand years ago, we "cross the Rubicon" every time we make a bold decision or take a step from which there is no retreat.

There was no retreat for Caesar. As he marched south through Italy, town after town welcomed him wildly. His legions were hailed as liberators, the road to Rome had never been so festively open. Nor was there any opposition when Caesar reached the gates of the great city. No troops came out to bar his way. Pompey and his followers had fled.

SPARTACUS

...The Slave Who Freed Himself

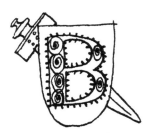ESIDES serving as favorite winter quarters for various battalions, the city of Capua was a lovely and fashionable resort near Naples. Among its attractions were pleasure gardens, elaborate parks, fanciful fountains whose marble basins held varieties of tropical fish, an air made fragrant by perfume manufactories, and a famous school for gladiators.

Gladiators were the most important product of Capua; they furnished the greatest thrills in the festival games in the Colosseum. They were slaves trained to fight and kill each other—the short sword with which they fought was called a *gladius*. Since there were three times as many slaves as free citizens in Rome, and since every war brought new prisoners who became slaves, there was always a ready supply of gladiators.

Unlike other slaves, gladiators were not overworked and undernourished; on the contrary they were kept sleek and strong to make a fine appearance in the arena. They were taught not only to put on a good performance, but to give and take fatal blows. In order to please the bloodthirsty spectators they had to learn how to fight fiercely and die handsomely. When a gladiator was wounded after a spirited combat, the onlookers might hold up their thumbs to show that his life should be spared. If they did not think well of his performance or were bored, they turned their thumbs down, and that was the end of the unfortunate contestant. The spirit of the times was cold and cruel. Roman crowds wanted constant excitement; in the arena they demanded violent action and were completely indifferent to bloodshed.

In 73 B. C. a Thracian slave did what was considered impossible:

134

he led a revolt of the gladiators and organized them so successfully that they almost overthrew Rome. His name was Spartacus. He never intended to conquer the country; all he wanted was to free himself of the hideous sport of fighting and killing his fellow slaves. With two others he planned an escape: the word was passed around until some fifty or more would be ready for the signal to break out. It happened one noon.

"It will be while we are eating," Spartacus whispered to Crixus, a captive from Gaul. "That is the time when the guards are most certain that we have no thoughts except about food. They would kill us before we raised a hand if they thought we were plotting escape. Romans have a contempt for life; I have a contempt for killing. But we will be forced to kill before we win our freedom. Tell Oenomaus to tell the others to watch when I drop my plate."

The mess hall seemed no different that day than any other day. The doors were not only shut but bolted; guards with whips, clubs, and swords walked among the tables, heavily armed soldiers were stationed outside the room. But there was something stirring in the mess hall that the slaves could not name but all of them understood. They were silent, not eating. They watched Spartacus. He dropped his plate and stood up.

"Here! What do you think you're doing!" yelled one of the guards. "Pick up that plate and sit down!"

Spartacus did not answer. He turned around, seized the guard by the throat and broke his neck. All the other gladiators sprang up as the guards ran toward Spartacus. They had no weapons, but they picked up benches and tables, and before the guards could snap a whip or draw a sword, they were attacked. The place was an uproar of struggling guards and gladiators; in a few minutes the guards were overcome, pinned down, and beaten to death. The gladiators swarmed into the kitchen, killed the cooks, and seized knives, cleavers, shears, even the spits. Then they broke down the doors and flew at the surprised soldiers who were lolling under the trees. They were outnumbered and easily outfought; the rest panicked and ran away. The gladiators put on the armor of the dead soldiers and within half an hour Spartacus and his followers marched out of Capua. On the road they overtook and captured a cart full of arms. They were now well equipped.

They found safety in a wood on the slopes of Mount Vesuvius. There Spartacus addressed them.

"We have fought our last fight against each other," he said. "We

are no longer gladiators. Nor are we slaves. We are free men. To keep our freedom we must stay together. We will find a place where we can stay free."

At first there were not more than sixty or seventy. But the few soon grew into a band of hundreds; they were joined by other runaway slaves and gladiators who had escaped from a dozen cities. Within six months Spartacus found himself the leader of an army of a hundred thousand of the hardiest soldiers who had ever faced an enemy.

The consuls and senators were outraged and astounded; outraged that a slave should dare to start an uprising, astounded that it should be so successful. They sent an army to put down the impudent rebellion. The army was defeated and Spartacus divided the armor among his men. The plain people of Rome were also startled but less alarmed. They were, in fact, thrilled—it was for them a kind of glorified gladiatorial combat on a mammoth scale.

Aroused and vindictive, the Roman authorities sent out a proclamation that Spartacus was a leader of a criminal gang and a huge reward was offered for his capture. In retaliation Spartacus issued a proclamation calling for the end of slavery. The pick of the legions were pitted against him, but the mixed horde of Thracians, Gauls, and other ex-slaves could not be beaten.

They would have remained invincible had they been, as Spartacus advised, united by a common purpose. He urged them to cross the Alps and find a home where they would not be pursued, where they could live the life of normal men. But dissension broke out among the men. Many of them preferred plunder to a general escape.

"Why should we leave Italy?" they said. "Let's stay here. It's a rich land, a fine place to loot."

To make matters worse, the Gauls grew jealous of the Thracians —"Spartacus came from Thrace," they said. "That's why he favors them"—and the Thracians looked down on the Gauls. His friend Crixus had been slain in battle; Oenomaus was deeply troubled. There were times when Spartacus was tempted to give up the leadership of his unruly forces and find peace elsewhere with the original small group of gladiators. But he had a task to perform, a mission to which he was now dedicated.

After two years of varied guerrilla tactics and open warfare Spartacus managed to keep his troops intact and bring them to the Gulf of Tarentum in the south of Italy. There they spent the winter, planning maneuvers, repairing old weapons and making new ones for the campaign to come. Spartacus knew it would be a decisive conflict; Rome was preparing to send its largest and most war-hardened legions to crush him.

Licinius Crassus was sent down from Rome in command of an overwhelming force. The legions attacked and succeeded in pushing Spartacus back as far as Reggio. There his band was held in the grip of a pincer movement between Crassus' army and the sea. He tried to escape the predicament by hiring boats to transport his men to Sicily—Sicily, rich in grain, was often called the bread-basket of Italy, and Spartacus hoped to humble Rome by cutting off its supply of flour. But the shipowners were either unable or unwilling to risk helping a slave who dared to challenge the power of the greatest empire on earth.

Crassus had hemmed him in. He had driven Spartacus' troops on to a narrow isthmus, where he had isolated them by digging wide ditches all along their lines. Spartacus did nothing; he was so inactive that Crassus was sure he had him trapped. Then, one stormy night when the snow whirled and blinded and no one could stand against the battering wind, Spartacus got his men to fill in the ditches, skirt around Crassus' camp, and reach the mainland. Crassus sent to Rome for reinforcements. They came, and once again Spartacus found himself fighting on two fronts. It was fiercer than any preceding battle; both sides had tremendous losses, and Spartacus suffered most. His ranks had been thinned during the long period when they were held at bay. But there were no cowards among them. Of the fifteen thousand men slain in combat, the only two of Spartacus' men who failed to face the enemy had been wounded in the back.

Spartacus was able to consolidate the rest of his army for another head-on conflict. This, he felt would be the final one. Oenomaus was beside him as they rode into battle. When they came close to the enemy, Spartacus dismounted and killed his horse.

"Why?" asked the astonished Oenomaus. "Why at this time?"

"If we win," answered Spartacus, "we shall have plenty of horses. If we lose, I shall need none. I will not live in defeat to be brought back into slavery."

It was sword against sword in a desperate attempt to reach Crassus. Spartacus slashed his way through the Roman ranks until he was surrounded. He called for Crassus to settle the issue hand to hand, but he was cut down. Even then he continued to fight on his knees. When the Romans searched for his body, it was found under a pile of the soldiers he had slain.

It had been an uneven struggle, a struggle not only against superior strength but also against cruelty and wrong. Six thousand of the captured slaves were crucified along the highway leading from Rome to Capua. In Spartacus' camp after his death, however, the three thousand prisoners were found unharmed. Spartacus was unable to overcome the brutality of the world in which he lived. But he did not die in vain. A slave who freed himself, he is remembered by all men for the liberty-loving spirit that will not die.

ANDROCLES

...The Slave Freed by a Lion

BOUT two thousand years ago there lived a teacher whose pupils adored him. His name was Apion, and he was so wrapped up in his studies he did not realize. that his pupils loved him not because he was so learned but because he told such marvelous tales. He told these tales with such skill that he could make his listeners believe the most unbelievable stories. His favorite and most famous one concerned a man who befriended a ferocious man-eating lion and who, in turn, was rescued by the savage beast. Apion claimed that the story was absolutely true; he said that he knew the man—and the lion, too.

The story begins in rough country, on a farm. There a slave worked night and day, hour after endless hour, for the governor of the colony, who was a cruel master. The slave's name was Androcles, and he was a small, careworn, kind and patient man. There seemed no limit to his patience. Overworked and underfed, he performed the hardest tasks without complaint. He had been born into slavery; he was the son of a slave and the grandson of a slave. Freedom for him was not even a hope. It was something of which he never dared to dream.

"Today," said his master, one summer morning, "you are to plow this ten-acre field that has never been plowed. It is rough and stony, but I can't spare any of the oxen now. So you will be the ox. You will get into harness and pull the plow yourself. One of the overseers will guide the plow and make sure you don't get any queer ideas into your head. That's all. Now get to work."

140

It was a broiling day in mid-July. The field was clogged with
boulders and matted with thorny vines. It was almost impossible to
cut and turn up the heavy soil. Androcles strained every muscle to
pierce and break up the resisting earth, but he made little progress.
At noon the sun was so intense that the overseer could not even
walk behind the panting Androcles any longer.

"You can rest a few minutes. I'll sit under this tree and watch
you," he said. "Better not try anything you'll be sorry for." He
sprawled out to eat his lunch and cool himself with a flask of wine.
Whether it was the heat of the day or the wine which made him
close his eyes, the overseer nodded, then his head drooped, and he
began to snore.

At that moment something happened to Androcles. He dreamed
the forbidden dream. The dream became a reality as he slipped out
of the harness and shook off the straps that held him to the plow.
He stood up straight. He lifted his head high, and it was no longer a
slave's head. He was free.

For a moment Androcles stood still; he did not know what to do
with his liberty. Then, without thinking, he began to run. He ran
unaware of what he was doing or where he was going. He ran over
fields, stumbled through hedges, jumped over walls, waded across
streams, plunged into thick woods. His heart pounded violently, but
he continued to run and run and run until he could not take another
step. When he fell he saw that he had fallen in front of a hollow, a
cave in the side of a hill. The cave was cool and dark; it looked
empty. Androcles had just strength enough to crawl inside. Then he
collapsed and sank into a dreamless, deathlike sleep.

When he awoke he did not know what had happened or how
he had got to wherever he was. The first thing he sensed was a
peculiar smell, a strong smell that seemed to belong to some animal.
Next his hearing came back; he listened to the birds waking each
other. Then he began to see dimly. Looking through the opening
he could see a thin light trickled into the cave. But suddenly the
light was blotted out—a huge and bristling form blacked out the
entrance.

The form was frightful. Androcles realized it was a monstrous
lion returning from his nightly prowl. Quaking, he shrank against
the wall. The lion stood there roaring. But it did not spring; it never
even bared its teeth. Androcles did not budge; he was bewildered.
Suddenly he ceased to fear for his life. It occurred to him that what

he thought was a roar of anger or a howl of hunger was a cry of pain. Trembling, the kind and patient man went up to the lion.

"Is something hurting you?" he inquired.

The lion groaned.

"I thought so," Androcles in a soothing voice. "Let's see what it is."

The lion lifted a huge, hairy paw.

"Oh, I see," sympathized Androcles. "That's it—a long, nasty thorn. No wonder it hurts. I'm surprised you can walk."

Full of self-pity, the lion moaned again. He moved a step closer.

"Now, don't be frightened," said Androcles, who was still trembling. "We'll see what we can do. It's going to hurt a little, but you must—er—grit your teeth. No biting, remember, and keep your claws to yourself. Now let's have the poor foot."

The lion, whimpering softly, held out the injured paw. Androcles took it in his hand, stroked it for a moment, and then tugged at the thorn. The lion pulled back and let out another roar, this time a roar of unmistakable rage.

"Now, now," said Androcles, "you mustn't talk like that to the doctor. You must be a big, brave lion, not a cowardly little cub. We'll have it all out the next try. Once more, now——ready?"

Androcles' fingers tightened around the thorn; the lion held still, his eyes shut, and suddenly the thorn was out.

"There," said Androcles, as the lion shook himself. "It didn't hurt so much, did it? Now let's see how it feels when you walk."

Gingerly the lion put the sore paw upon the ground; he took a cautious step or two. Then he bounded up to Androcles and licked his face.

Then the two of them settled down comfortably and went to sleep.

Life with the lion was a continual pleasure. There was no question as to who was the master and who was the slave. There was not even a distinction between man and beast. They were companions, friends in the forest, safe, secure, and serene in their happiness. They managed to be well nourished with a variety of food. Every morning the lion would bring home his kill—a plump rabbit, a young deer, or perhaps a wild turkey—and Androcles would catch fish and gather berries, which he taught the lion to like. It was a rare thing, this understanding between a naturally wild creature and the man who had gone back to nature. The two were united by a bond of mutual

respect and something more, something close to love. They roamed
the woods, swam streams and, after Androcles had cooked the meal,
sat about the fire together. Androcles talked, and the lion listened
attentively, purring to show he agreed with every word.

Things went on like this for a long while—a year, two years,
three years. Androcles could not tell, for he had stopped counting
the days. Then the companionship came to a sudden end. One afternoon Androcles was tempted to stray a little beyond the forest toward an orchard where fruit was ripening. There he heard a sound
that alarmed him more than the roaring of any animal. It was the
sound of human voices. Androcles turned to run back to the haven
of his cave. But it was too late. There were six armed men searching
for fugitive slaves. They spread out, cut off his retreat, and captured
him without a struggle.

"A dirty looking specimen," grumbled the leader. "More like a
beast than a man. I've half a mind to let him go. No one would
want him around the house, not even in the workrooms."

"There can't be too many slaves, and we can't be too particular,"
said one of the other men. "Besides, those who aren't fit for work
can be used for sport in the arena."

"That's so," replied the leader. "The Emperor has just declared
another big holiday—free bread and circuses for everybody—and,"
he laughed unpleasantly, "free food for the wild beasts in the
Colosseum."

They snapped the chains on Androcles.

Months went by. Androcles, with other runaway slaves, had been
brought to Rome. He was kept in a locked room, a kind of cavern
underneath the building where the games were held. He did not
know what was to become of him.

The Colosseum was crowded to the last seat: fifty thousand
spectators had come to witness their favorite spectacle. They had
been promised a gala Roman holiday, and they cheered lustily when
the Emperor, robed in purple, entered the royal platform and seated
himself on the imperial couch. All the first-ranking nobles were
there: Senators, Pontiffs, Magistrates, and also the holy Vestals. The
Emperor raised his hand and the performance began.

First there was a parade to dazzle the eye and indicate the excitement to come. At the head of the procession, accompanied by a
military band, marched the Praetorian Guard, the Emperor's own
soldiers, clad in scarlet embroidered with gold. There followed the

captains of the regular army in shining armor, regiments newly arrived from abroad carrying their trophies, embattled veterans and beardless young volunteers. A different band separated the conquered: prisoners of foreign wars, men and women to be sold into slavery, traitors and captured slaves to be put to death. Some shambled past, with their eyes on the dust; others, in spite of the chains, carried their heads high. But all knew that the drums were pronouncing their doom. This was the part of the spectacle that the crowd enjoyed least. Although it displayed the power of Rome, people were glad when it was over and the gay part of the pageant could be resumed.

There was a new burst of music as the gladiators swept into the amphitheatre. Those on foot flourished their swords and bucklers; those in chariots whipped up the horses, while their brilliantly colored scarves streamed into the wind. Then came the other combatants: retiarii with nets to entangle their victims and with tridents to stab them; fire-throwers, spear-hurlers, lancers, archers with bows and arrows.

Last of all came the beasts: elephants who would be pitted against horned rhinoceri; bears trained to attack buffalo; wild horses that would be matched against savage boars; bulls that would be goaded and killed by men waving pieces of red cloth. The only animals missing were the lions—these were too ferocious to be let loose, for they had been confined in dark pits and starved for days to make them more bloodthirsty.

There was a fanfare of trumpets and the parade stopped. All the combatants faced the Emperor's box and, raising their right hands, cried as with one voice: "Hail, Caesar! We who are ready to die salute thee!"

Then the games began. They began harmlessly enough with a series of chariot races (the deadly gladiatorial combats were always kept for the climax) and the spectators cheered their favorites. Every charioteer had his group of admirers; the horses too had their ardent followers. Exhibitions of skill and danger came next: Egyptians juggling naked swords, swords so sharpened that they could cut to the bone; wrestlers, their bodies smeared with oil tossing each other about in a small square lined with knives, boxers wearing brass knuckles studded with nails; bowmen who used small torches instead of arrows on targets that were running human beings.

An intermission allowed attendants to mop up the blood, strew fresh sand and carry off the dead and dying, while the onlookers refreshed themselves with wine and sweet drinks. Then, as a diversion before the struggles of man against man and beast against beast, a few runaway slaves were to be thrown to the lions. The first of those chosen was Androcles.

Thrust into the middle of the colossal arena, he stood pitifully small. He had been given a cudgel, but it was so puny a defense against a starved and ravenous lion that it seemed an added cruelty. He stood up straight—he had been free—at least he would not die like a slave grovelling on the ground. Hearing a gate being swung back on its hinges, he closed his eyes. He heard a tremendous roar, but he did not watch the lion coming for its prey. He did not see the lion leaping furiously across the sand. Nor did he understand why the lion suddenly stopped and the spectators grew quiet. In the hush he was aware of a curious sniffing and he felt something rubbing against his ankles. He opened his eyes—and could not believe them. For there was the lion—his lion—brushing a paw against his clothes, fawning on him, standing up to lick his face, purring and rolling over with joy.

The crowd went wild. "Magnificent!" "Marvellous!" "A miracle!" they shouted, holding out fists with the thumbs pressed back to ask that the man's life be spared. The Emperor stood up. A life, especially the life of a slave, lost or saved, meant nothing to him, but he liked the approval of the crowd.

"Come here," he called to Androcles. "You are either a brave man or a lucky one. Or you are a magician. It does not matter to me. But it seems to matter to my people. They want you to live. So you shall be my Chief Keeper of Animals."

"Oh, your majesty, I couldn't do that," said Androcles. "Thank you all the same, but I couldn't. I—I am afraid of animals."

The Emperor smiled. "That is amusing enough to earn you something extra. This great beast here acts as though he were your loyal, long-lost dog. Would you, perhaps, like to be set up in business as a doctor of pets? It's a pleasant way of living, I'm told, and profitable, too."

"Thank you again, your majesty, but no. There's only one thing I would like to do."

"And what is that?" asked the Emperor.

"I would like to go back to the forest, and live there—with the lion, of course."

"If that is all—and it is little enough—you are free to go, free in every sense. The gods have been kind to a slave, and I, who do their bidding, can do no less. Go," said the Emperor, "and our protection goes with you."

Side by side, Androcles and the lion left the arena. Out of the Colosseum they walked through the streets of Rome, while people wondered at the strange sight. Out of the city they went, then across the fields, and into the forest. There they were again, good companions, fellow-creatures, free, happy, and at home.

BOADICEA

...The Warrior Queen

NDER Caesar's leadership the Romans had extended their conquests into Britain. But, after Caesar withdrew his troops for more victories in Europe, the island was left alone, and for a hundred years the natives were allowed to govern themselves. Rome would never willingly give up her gains, however, and in the year 43 A. D. the Emperor Claudius determined to recapture Britain and colonize it. After the Roman legions had gained a foothold, Claudius himself arrived at the head of an army and appointed a Roman governor to rule the island.

The Britons resisted bravely; they did not give up the uneven struggle but fought fiercely with primitive weapons. The poorly organized tribes could not, however, withstand the attacks of trained soldiers; their camps were burned and their forts destroyed. Even when defeated, they would not bow down to the Romans. One of the captives, a Welsh chief by the name of Caradoc, simply refused to kneel to the Romans, and the Emperor Claudius, who admired courage, set him free.

Because of the Britons' ceaseless resistance, the Roman rule in Britain grew harsher. Finally it became heartless. The Britons were treated like slaves, beaten unmercifully, and robbed of their possessions. One of the British chiefs hoped to persuade the invaders to abandon their cruel tactics by offering them half of all his property, including horses and cattle; the other half was to be held by his wife Boadicea and his children, under the protection of the Emperor. But as soon as the chief died, the Romans seized the property he had left to his family. With her two daughters, Boadicea went on foot to the Roman governor.

"Is this just?" she complained. "When my husband was living, he made a fair distribution of everything he owned. You then promised to respect his position as king of the Iceni and protect his family. Now I have become the chief of our tribe, and I ask, is this the way to treat a queen?"

"A queen?" sneered the governor. "You are nothing but an ignorant woman who doesn't know enough to hold her tongue. You are not only ignorant but impudent, like all your people. I shall show you how you should be treated. Here," he called to his guards. "Take this woman and show her how we treat people who talk too much."

The soldiers took Boadicea to the market-place and, in front of the townspeople, beat her with rods. When her two daughters tried to protect her, they too were whipped.

Boadicea had been shamed, but her sense of outrage was far stronger than her humiliation. That night she summoned the heads of her tribe.

"What has happened to me," she said, "can happen to any of you —all of you. And it *will* happen if we act like the weaklings the Romans believe we are. Are we cowards? Will we live as slaves? Or will we stand up and fight—and if we have to, die—so that we can live or die as free men? We have been driven too far. It is time for us to fight back. Let us drive the Romans out of the country."

A week later, the Iceni, joined by neighboring tribes, attacked the governor's camp. The greater part of the Roman army was fighting in Wales, and Queen Boadicea had little trouble disposing of the relatively small garrison. She was a glorious figure as she plunged into combat. Taller than most of her countrywomen, she stood splendidly erect in her chariot, her yellow hair falling to her waist and her blue eyes blazing with passion. She wore a wide gold collar around her neck, and the wind made her dark purple cloak fly from her shoulders like the wings of some great bird. Followed by her daughters, she led wild charges against the enemy. Disdaining any attempt to outwit or encircle them, she flew straight at their center.

One Roman encampment after another crumbled under her attack. Flushed with a growing sense of power, Boadicea swept on to London, at that time little more than a Roman fort. In revenge for the wrongs they had suffered, her hot-headed followers set fire to the houses and drove out the inhabitants.

Bold though the Britons were, they were not able to sweep the hated foreigners from their shores. The Romans returned from

Wales stronger than ever. Except for Boadicea's tribes, there were no other British armies opposing them. Boadicea knew this would be the final conflict. She addressed her men solemnly.

"Tomorrow will tell whether we are to belong to Rome or to ourselves. Those of you who are willing to submit to the invaders, go back to your homes. Those who remain must be ready to die for the homes they may never see again. We are Britain's last hope."

The next day brought the end of that hope. Boadicea's men fought savagely and recklessly——it is said that they fought with their nails and teeth like wild animals. Though they broke through the enemy's lines, in the end they were no match for the superior arms and organization of the Roman army. The Britons were beaten and forced to flee to the forest.

Boadicea would not run and hide. Neither would she stay to be captured and enslaved by the Romans. She had resolved never to give herself up, and she always carried with her a deadly poison. Now, with a last cry of defiance, she swallowed it.

OGIER THE DANE

...How He Saved Charlemagne's Life

 F all the followers of Charlemagne, Emperor of France, none was more faithful than Ogier. He was not one of Charlemagne's countrymen. On the contrary, Ogier's father, King of Denmark, had defied Charlemagne, had been defeated and forced to deliver his son to the emperor as a hostage.

Making Ogier an underling seemed to put a stop to all the great things and glorious career that had been predicted for Ogier when he was still an infant. A few days after he was born six noble sisters came to his cradle. They had the power of prophecy and they all promised to protect Ogier.

"You shall be the bravest of warriors," said the first. "You shall have the keen eye of the eagle, the strength of the tiger, and the courage of the lion."

"You shall have many adventures, many chances to prove your valor," said the second.

"You shall not only be brave but unbeaten," said the third. "No foe shall ever conquer you."

"A brave heart and a stout arm are all very well," said the fourth. "But you shall have more than power over men. You shall gain their respect and their love."

"These are all great gifts, but they may prove dangerous. They may make you proud and selfish. Therefore I say you shall respect those who respect you, and you shall return their love."

"My sisters have wished wonderful things for you," said the sixth. "But they have said nothing about your term of life. I say you shall live until you have accomplished everything you desire, you shall become one of the knights at King Arthur's round table, and your name shall live long after your death."

All went well until Ogier was almost sixteen years old. Then troubles descended on him. His father, King Geoffroy of Denmark, had refused to pay tribute to Charlemagne. When Charlemagne invaded Denmark and compelled the Danes to acknowledge him as their sovereign, he demanded a royal hostage to insure their sincerity. After the death of Ogier's mother, Geoffroy had remarried, and Ogier was hated by his stepmother, who had a son of her own. Planning to have her son inherit the crown, she saw this as an opportunity to get Ogier out of the country.

"You can save Denmark and yourself at the same time," she said slyly to Geoffroy. "There is no one more royal than Ogier, and Charlemagne would be glad to have him. Moreover, it would be good for your son. He would become part of the great emperor's household and receive a splendid education at the French court."

So Ogier was brought up in Charlemagne's court. He was popular from the moment he arrived. His noble bearing and courteous manner impressed everyone. He became friends with the young comrades, Roland and Oliver. Charlemagne looked upon him with special favor. It grieved Ogier that his father never sent for him and that, until he would be acknowledged as a prince and became a knight, he was still a hostage.

When the Saracens landed in Italy, and Rome and the Church were in danger, Charlemagne set out to the aid of Pope Leo. The Emperor took not only his army but also his entire court with him. The opposing armies met near Rome. Ogier, riding at Roland's side, was unhappy because he was still a squire and too young to take an active part in the conflict.

"It was said that I would have the eyes of an eagle and the courage of a lion. But what good are these things when I cannot distinguish myself in arms. I would willingly die carrying the royal Oriflamme into battle."

"Your time will come," said Roland. "I, too, woud give my life to bear the red Oriflamme, that holy banner whose streamers look like living flames. But it is borne by the knight Alory. Alory claims it because he is of the Pope's party, yet he is unworthy of the honor. I distrust him. Let's watch what he does."

What Alory did was unspeakable. When the Saracens charged, he fled. He lowered the Oriflamme and dragged it along the ground.

"Shame!" cried Ogier and Roland in one breath. They stopped Alory in his flight. Roland seized the horse and Ogier struck Alory down. Then they disarmed the coward. Roland took his sword, while Ogier picked up the Oriflamme and put on Alory's armor.

Mounting Alory's horse, he cried "Follow me!" to the retreating troops. "Those of you who have lost your weapons, use whatever is lying on the field—discarded daggers, lances, even sticks and stones! But follow!"

Seeing the Oriflamme flying into the front of the battle lines, Charlemagne's men rallied. Although surrounded by Saracens, they held fast. Suddenly a group of Saracen knights plunged through to where Charlemagne was fighting and unhorsed him. They knew who he was and were making ready to deliver the death-blow when Ogier came to his rescue. Using the Oriflamme as a lance, he swung and thrust it so powerfully that he broke the sword of one of the Saracens, knocked down another, and pierced the throat of a third. The rest fled.

"My good Alory," said Charlemagne, rising to his feet. "I owe my life to you."

Ogier said nothing· and, bowing deeply, was about to withdraw when one of Charlemagne's captains stopped him.

"What happened?" he asked. "There's something queer about this. A little while ago we saw you running from the field, about to throw away the Oriflamme as though it were a worthless burden. And now you lay it at our leader's feet in triumph."

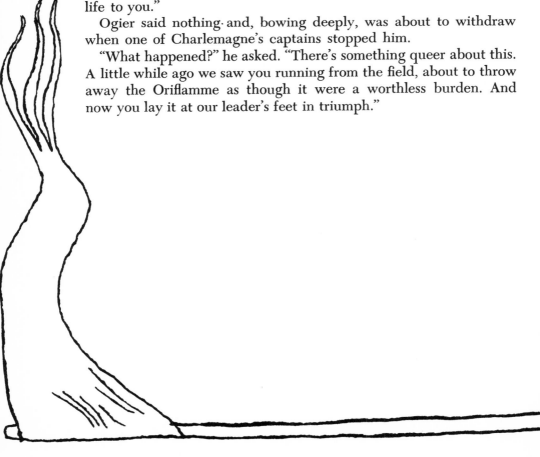

"That's right," said Charlemagne. "I, too, wonder at you and what you have done. Here you are, short in stature, walking ill at ease in armor too large for you. I would like to see the face of the man who accepted defeat as his doom and then turned defeat into victory. What kind of coward suddenly becomes a hero? Alory, take off your helmet. I want to look at you."

Charlemagne stared in amazement as Ogier threw off Alory's helmet and knelt before the emperor.

"Unbelievable!" said Charlemagne. "A boy——and you have saved my life! But the surprise has almost stopped my heart. Let me embrace you, my son, for my son you shall be. Since you are still kneeling, remain in that position another moment."

He turned to one of his squires. "Give me my sword Joyeuse," he said. Then laying it lightly on Ogier's shoulder, he spoke solemnly.

"This sword is a sacred thing. It is both a weapon and a symbol, and it is proud to welcome you to my company of knights. Ogier the Dane is now no longer a hostage. He is one of the brotherhood of valiant knights. He has the true temper, the strength, and the surety of this matchless steel. Rise now, Sir Ogier."

And Chalemagne gave Ogier the invincible sword Joyeuse.

ROLAND AND OLIVER

... *No Greater Love*

OLAND and Ogier were good companions, but Roland's dearest friend and closest comrade was Oliver. The two men did not begin as friends but as enemies.

For months the emperor Charlemagne had besieged the city of Vienne which was held by Count Gerard. The town was so heavily fortified and so well supplied that it seemed able to hold out forever. At times the defenders made raids upon the encamped enemy troops and tried to throw them back; at other times Charlemagne's soldiers stormed the town in force. Neither side could gain an advantage.

One day while a group of Charlemagne's men were practicing swordsmanship, a young knight rode into their midst. He was richly armed, his shield blood-red, and the plume on his helmet bright scarlet. The men assumed he was from another part of the camp and, when he asked to join in their sport, they welcomed him. It soon became evident that he outmatched all the others in skill with the sword and also with the lance. Having won all the matches, he was about to ride off when one of the soldiers stopped him.

"You cannot get away that easy," he said. "You haven't faced our best man."

"Who is that?" asked the knight in red.

"Our emperor's nephew, Roland, of course," replied the man. "They call him 'the Achilles of the West.' He is the first of Charlemagne's ten champions and he would be happy to cross swords with you."

The two met on the practice field and dueled with every kind of weapon. But neither could surpass the other. Finally Roland asked the stranger for his name.

157

"You must be one of the new reinforcements," said Roland. "I haven't seen you before. Where are you from?"

Instead of replying, the red knight leaped on his horse and dug his spurs in the horse's flank.

"He's not one of ours!" shouted Roland. "After him!"

But the stranger was too quick. He was out of the camp in a flash, galloping swiftly toward Vienne. Even the fastest of Charlemagne's riders could not catch up with him.

Time passed slowly. Both the besieged and the besiegers began to suffer. The farms had been depleted of food, the woods were being cut down for firewood. To make matters worse, news reached Charlemagne that Marsilius, the Spanish king and ally of the Saracens, was leading a pagan army through southern France and laying waste that rich and lovely countryside. Many of Charlemagne's counsellors were for giving up the siege of Vienne and making peace with Gerard. But Charlemagne was not only a proud monarch but a stubborn one.

"I have sworn to punish this disloyal Gerard," he declared. "I will teach him that a subject cannot oppose his lord. I will do so even if it means losing half my army."

"You don't have to make so great a sacrifice," said Ganelon, his chief adviser. "You can bring this impasse to an end the same way the warring Greeks and Trojans resolved many of their differences."

"What way was that?" asked Charlemagne.

"They let one hero from each side represent his army. You, too, can choose a champion to represent our side," answered Ganelon, "while Gerard does the same. The two knights then meet in single combat and decide the issue between them. There is no question that your nephew Roland will win."

When the matter was proposed to Count Gerard, he too was in favor of the plan. The siege had exhausted his supplies as well as the patience of his people and he was glad to leave the decision to fate. Time and place were agreed upon, and next day the two knights chosen for the combat met on a meadow situated near the banks of the river Rhône. Roland arrived first. A few minutes later he was startled when the opposing paladin arrived. It was the knight of the red shield and scarlet plume.

"You asked my name," said the champion from Vienne. "But I was too much in a hurry then to stop for courtesies. I will tell you now. My name is Oliver. I am Count Gerard's nephew and you are the nephew of our enemy. We nephews seem to be well matched."

"We shall see how well matched we are," said Roland. "Mount your horse."

The crowds drawn up on either side cheered loudly as the two handsome young knights spurred their steeds forward. They met in the middle of the meadow and their lances splintered as they struck furiously against each other's shields. Though the shock was great, neither was thrown from his horse. Both men dismounted quickly and faced each other on foot.

"Swords now," said Roland, drawing his weapon from its sheath.

"Mine is ready," said Oliver. "Parry this blow if you can."

For an hour it was stroke and counterstroke, blow upon blow. Neither contestant was injured, neither yielded an inch. Then Roland delivered so powerful a thrust that Oliver's shield was split in two and his sword broken. From the defenders of Vienne rose a great cry of distress as Oliver stood, head upright, waiting for the death-blow. But Roland lowered his sword.

"I would never sleep for shame if I slew an unarmed man," he said. "Let us match swords again. It is only fair that you should try mine, while I take another blade."

Either because Roland's sword was made of finer steel, or because it was Oliver's turn to get in a telling blow, the fighting took a new turn. In a series of thrusts and parries, the sword Roland was using was struck from his hand and, falling on a rock, it broke in two.

"You are now the defenseless one," said Oliver. "I give you your life as you gave me mine. Swords do not seem to decide for us. However, one of us must get the better of the other. What do you say?"

"I say yes," said Roland. "And I propose we fight it out with clubs."

They clubbed each other for hours to no avail. When the clubs were thrown aside, the two men fought with their fists. Then they wrestled but, though they tumbled each other ingloriously on the ground, there was no victory for either. They stood up. It was growing dark.

"It is a mad thing we are doing," said Roland. "By now it must be plain that neither of us can win over the other. We are perfectly matched and were not meant to be enemies, but friends. Give me your hand, good Oliver."

"Gladly," said Oliver. "Any man would be fortunate indeed to have a friend like you, Roland. Never have I seen a braver man, and never again will I lift a weapon against you."

Both sides rejoiced to see their valiant heroes embrace each other, knowing that both were unequalled in courage and honor. Charlemagne was deeply moved.

"Come," he said to Gerard. "Let us take an example from these gallant youths. They are already friends. They will become like brothers—at least they will be brothers-in-arms. There is no greater love. They have pledged their faith to each other. If you will swear to be loyal, I will be your friend and defender. Then we can end this senseless strife."

"I will so swear," replied Gerard. "Peace is better than fighting. Besides, we have a common cause. I will be proud to unite with you against Marsilius. I am—and will be—your man. Meanwhile, the gates of Vienne stand open for you and yours."

For three days there was much feasting in Gerard's castle. Charlemagne and Gerard sat at one end of the table, while Roland and Oliver sat at the other. From the moment they refused to continue fighting each other, Roland and Oliver were inseparable. Wherever they went, they lived together. And at the terrible battle of Roncesvalles, when Ganelon betrayed his emperor, they died together.

HOW ARTHUR BECAME KING

...*The Sword in the Stone*

T his death in the sixth century, England was without a king. The mighty king Uther Pendragon had died. The country was in great danger. Knights quarreled among themselves, barons threatened to seize London; every lord hoped to snatch the crown for himself. In this crisis the people turned to Merlin. Merlin had the reputation of being a wonderworker, a magician who was also a man of wisdom. He went to the archbishop and advised him to send for all the knights, the lords, and the barons to come to London at Christmas. There they would behold a miracle. Moreover, the miracle would show them who was to be king of England.

When all the high-ranking men had assembled in front of St. Paul's Cathedral they saw a strange sight. In the churchyard stood a large square stone. In it there was an anvil of steel sunk into the stone, and at the very center was a naked sword. Carved on the stone were letters of gold which read:

> *Whoso pulleth this sword out of this stone and anvil
> is the rightly born king of England.*

Everyone marvelled, and when the church service was over, all those who hoped to be king tried to pull the sword from the stone, but none could loosen it. Even the strongest could not make it stir.

"It is evident that the man is not here who can lift that sword," said the archbishop. "But no doubt God will make the right man known at the right time. Meanwhile, let us appoint ten knights of good fame to keep guard over this wondrous thing."

162

"Meanwhile, too," added Merlin, "let all the lords prepare themselves for another attempt. On New Year's Day a tournament will be held. Any knight who wishes may enter; perhaps then it will be made known which one will win the sword and the kingdom."

On New Year's Day a great array of knights and barons rode to the tournament. Among them were the well-liked Sir Ector, his son Sir Kay, and Arthur, who was Kay's young foster-brother.

As they neared the field, Kay clapped a hand against his forehead. "At least my head is still here," he said ruefully. "But I must be losing my mind. Last night I unbuckled my sword as usual and placed it against the door. This morning I was in such a hurry to get to the tournament I forgot to put it on again."

"Let me get it for you," said Arthur. "It won't take long."

But when Arthur reached home the doors were locked. Everyone had gone to see the tourney, and there was no way to get into the house.

"No matter," said Arthur to himself. "There is that sword in the churchyard. Perhaps I can slip by the knights who guard it."

He did not have to worry about the knights; they, too, were off to the tournament. Tying his horse to a tree, Arthur went into the churchyard, found the stone, and, too much in a hurry to read the written words, without the slightest effort he lifted the sword out of it. Then he rode rapidly to the field and gave the sword to Kay.

Kay knew immediately it was not his own sword. He knew what it was and he knew how it had been obtained. But he said nothing about Arthur when he showed it to his father.

"Here," he said, "is the sword from the stone. Therefore I am meant to be king of England. Am I not?"

Sir Ector made no answer to this. Instead he said, "The three of us will ride back to the church. There is something we must find out."

When they alighted he made Kay take an oath as to how he got the sword. Kay kept silent for several minutes. Then he replied, "My brother brought it to me."

"And how did *you* get it?" Sir Ector inquired of Arthur.

"There was no one at home to give me Kay's sword," said Arthur. "So I came here and pulled the sword out of the stone."

"Put it back in its place," said Sir Ector. When Arthur had done this, Sir Ector turned to Kay. "Now," he said, "draw it out."

Kay tugged at the sword with all his might, but it would not budge.

"Now," said Sir Ector to Arthur, "let us see how you did it."

"I did nothing in particular," said Arthur, "I just pulled lightly—like this—and the sword came out."

Sir Ector fell on his knees and forced Kay down too.

"What is the meaning of this?" cried the astonished Arthur. "Why, my own dear father and brother, do you kneel to me?"

"Because you are the rightful king who has made the miracle come true. And because I am not your father."

"Not my father?" echoed Arthur. "Then who is?"

"That, alas, I don't know," said Sir Ector. "You were brought to us by Merlin when you were a newborn infant. You were wrapped in a cloth of gold, and Merlin told us you were the child of a noble family and that we were to care for you. But he would not tell us why, nor would he say who your people were. He said that all would be known at the right time. That time must be near, for the sword proves you are to be our king. And when you are king I hope you will be gracious to us."

"If I am to be king," said Arthur, "I will not be able to do enough for you. And for my brother, too. He shall be steward of all my lands. But when will I learn who I really am?"

"Let us seek Merlin," said Sir Ector.

Hardly had he uttered these words when Merlin appeared.

"You need not tell me what happened," said Merlin. "The sword tells me all. But Arthur will not get his kingdom until the lords are satisfied that he is the rightly born king. We must wait until Candlemas when all the knights and barons will meet here. Meanwhile, put the sword back into the stone."

Candlemas came, and all the lords of the realm gathered before the stone. But no one could draw out the sword. Then Arthur lifted it easily and held it over his head. Still the lords were not satisfied.

"England is too great a country to be governed by a boy," they grumbled, "Especially an unknown boy. The whole thing is a trick!"

Merlin smiled. "There is no hurry. You can try again at Easter."

Easter came, but the lords did no better than at Candlemas.

"You shall have one more chance," said Merlin, "and that will be the last. We shall put it off until the feast of Pentecost."

At Pentecost, even though it became plain that no one but Arthur could move the sword, the lords still refused to give in.

"We would rather have no king at all," they complained, "than be ruled by a boy of common blood."

"Set your minds at ease," said Merlin. "His blood is better than that of any man here. It is the best blood in the land. I shall tell you a tale I had sworn never to tell until the proper moment. It begins before this boy was born. King Uther Pendragon had been in trouble and in poor health for some time; when his only son came into the world, he felt he could not protect him. Nor could his wife care for him, for she too was ill. To save the child from those who would do away with him and seize the throne, the king made me promise to deliver him secretly to the most faithful of his followers, Sir Ector and his wife. They would watch over him and bring him up as their own. He now stands before you with the sword in his hand. This is your king. Bow down to him!"

All the lords fell to their knees. They cried, "It is God's will! We will have Arthur for our king!" Then they asked pardon for their delay.

Arthur laid the sword upon the altar, and the archbishop, declaring he was a king of the purest blood, put the crown upon his head.

After the coronation, Arthur swore to govern with justice and mercy, to care for the poor and clear the land of wrong-doing. He designed a round table, so that when he dined with his knights, there was no head nor foot, but everyone seated had equal rank. No one ever questioned his gentleness or his goodness. He remained a benign and beloved king until the end of his life.

ALFRED THE GREAT

... The King, the Cakes, and the Beggar

 N the fifth century Rome was seriously threatened by so many barbarian tribes that its armies had to be called home. As soon as the Roman legions were withdrawn from Britain, the island was attacked by savage clans from Scotland and Ireland and invaded by Jutes, Angles, and Saxons from Europe. For three hundred years Britain was a battleground of rival leaders—at one time there were as many as seven different kingdoms among the Anglo-Saxons in Essex, Wessex, Sussex, Kent, East Anglia, Mercia, and Northumberland. When Alfred became king in 871 he was challenged by a new menace: the roving Danes, who sailed in low black ships and called themselves the kings of the sea.

Alfred had never expected to be a warrior; his father, King Ethelwulf, thought he would be a scholar or possibly a priest. Alfred's mother had died when he was four years old and, when he was seven, his father had taken him to see the Pope in Rome. On the return voyage, Ethelwulf had married Judith, a French princess. She was only eight years older than Alfred and proved to be a kind stepmother who took over his education.

Judith had brought with her a large, richly decorated book written by hand on parchment—this was hundreds of years before the invention of the printing press. It was illuminated with figures in many colors enriched with gold. She showed it to Alfred and his two older brothers. They looked at it curiously.

"Beautiful, isn't it?" she said. "The first one who can read it shall have it. Who will be the first to try?"

The two older brothers were not interested; they were too busy with bows and arrows. Alfred was shy, but he came closer and touched the manuscript.

"May I take it with me for a little while?" he asked.

His stepmother smiled. "Here it is," she said.

A few weeks later he brought the book back. Slowly and very carefully he read the lines of the first page.

"I do not know what all the words mean, but they have a wonderful sound," he said.

"They do indeed," said Judith, "for they are the words of God."

Alfred was twenty-two when, his father and brothers having died in battle, he became king. By this time the Danes had taken over large parts of Britain. They had proved their title of "kings of the sea" by sailing their ships in the most turbulent storms. Their blood-red flag was painted with the figure of a raven, and when the wind tossed the banner, the Danes would cry, "The raven claps its wings. It is a sign! We are bound to win!"

Win they did. Alfred was not a man of war. He fought for his countrymen as well as for his kingdom, but he fought halfheartedly. The struggle went on for seven years until the Danes were everywhere and Alfred had to flee for his life.

He became a wanderer. For a while he hid in the swamps at Somerset. Then, when spring came, he stayed in the woods, living on whatever could be hunted or found growing on trees and bushes. One day in late autumn he came to a woodcutter's house and asked for lodging.

"You can stay here a night or two," said the woodcutter's wife, "if you will attend to the cakes that are on the stove. Be sure to turn them over when one side gets brown. I must bring water from the well, so watch them carefully. See that they do not burn."

Alfred sat at the hearth, mending his bow. He dreamed of an army that could outfight the Danes. He dreamed of ruling in peace over a united Britain. He did not notice the smell of burning or the smoke that began to fill the room until the woodcutter's wife returned.

"You idle, good-for-nothing day-dreamer!" she screamed. "The cakes are ruined! Not a crumb will you get! Out you go!" Still scolding, she drove Alfred from the house.

"She was right," said Alfred to himself as she shut the door. "If I cannot watch over my people better than I watched the cakes, I am not fit to be king."

Still wandering in the forest, he found a deserted hovel. It seemed a safe hiding-place. Alfred had learned to take care of himself; but it was a poor hunting season, there were no berries on the bushes, no fruit on the trees, and he had little to eat.

It was an early winter evening when a beggar came to his door and begged a bite of food and shelter against the coming snow.

"I am as poor as you," said Alfred. "But there are some rushes in the corner where you may sleep. As for food, a loaf of bread is all I have. It is not much, but, such as it is, I will gladly share it with you."

Both men ate, talked for a while, and then went to sleep. Alfred dreamed again. This time he dreamed that a voice was telling him his troubles were coming to an end, that his men had been waiting to find him, and he would soon lead them again.

When he woke the beggar was gone. There was no sign that he had ever been there: the rushes had not been slept on and the portion of bread that Alfred had put out for him was untouched. As he sat wondering, a group of men burst in.

"We have found you at last!" they cried. "Something told us you might be in this part of the woods. We come with food for a king— game and fish and fruit. And we come with better than that. We come to tell you that an army is waiting for you a few miles from here."

One month later Alfred had organized his men. A bridge was thrown across the swamp, towers were built, and what had been a waste land was now a strong encampment. Nevertheless, he was not ready to attack.

"Before we challenge the Danes we must know something about their strength," he said. "We must find out how many men there are, how they are grouped, and where they are placed."

Knowing that the Danes were fond of songs and ballads, he disguised himself as a ballad-singer and was admitted to the enemy's camp. He was welcomed by Guthrun, the Danish commander.

"Minstrels are a happy relief in time of war," said Guthrun. "Take up your harp and sing to us. Let us hear some of the songs you have picked up on your travels."

Alfred played and sang—and observed. He saw how many soldiers there were, how they were armed, and where the camp could be most easily assaulted. Guthrun thanked him, gave him a gift, and Alfred returned to his men. A week later he attacked.

Alfred's army came out of the forest and stormed the weak point

of the Danish camp. Though they were outnumbered, Alfred's men fought off the enemy troops and then drove them back into the camp. For three weeks the Danes were surrounded and penned in. Then, seeing that his army was running short of food and water, Guthrun called for a truce. Alfred granted it.

When Guthrun was brought before King Alfred, he did not recognize him. Then Alfred showed him the gift and took up his harp.

"You have outfought us," said Guthrun. "But," he added with a wry smile, "first you had to outwit us. And now what are you going to do with us?"

"I am going to make you stop being the enemy," said Alfred. "Some time ago I learned a lesson about sharing. Instead of breaking the country into pieces between us, I would be willing to share it with you."

"A generous offer," said Guthrun. "One I am happy to accept. Here is my hand—and my heart, too. Now let us not talk as commanders but as friends."

There were many talks, all of them good. Guthrun divided Britain with Alfred. The north went to the Danes, the south to the Britons. A genuine understanding was established. There were no more battles or burnings. The Danes were now good neighbors and Guthrun became a Christian.

As in his youth, Alfred was once again a man of peace. He brought scholars and learned men to his court. He rebuilt towns that had been ruined by the war and founded schools for the poor. He translated Latin books into the language of the people and made laws that offered justice to all. His subjects venerated him, and Alfred the Great became Alfred the Good.

CANUTE THE WISE

... *The Rising Tide*

FTER the death of the Great and Good King Alfred, Britain was ruled by his descendants and also by various kings of Norway and Denmark. Finally it was united under the leadership of King Canute, son of a Dane who had married an Englishwoman. He was what the country needed. He stopped the tribes from warring on each other, built many churches, and established peace throughout the land.

In spite of his wisdom, Canute's courtiers were afraid of him. They remembered he was of fierce Danish stock, and because of their fear they flattered him. There was no limit to their flattery.

"O king," one would say, "there is no one as mighty as you in the whole world."

"O king, there is nothing you cannot do," another would echo.

"O king, you are not only ruler of the world," still another would say. "You are also monarch of the universe. Everything obeys you."

Finally Canute could not bear to listen to the foolish flattery any longer. One day, when the king and his courtiers were at Southampton on the south coast of England, he thought of a way to rebuke them.

"You think I am the mightiest of the mighty?" he asked the courtiers bowing before him. "You think everyone and everything must obey me?"

"O yes, your majesty," they replied, bowing still lower.

"Well, let us see," he said. "Bring me my chair and we will go down to the shore."

Puzzled, the courtiers carried the chair over the sands.

"Closer to the water," said the king. "You will notice, gentlemen, that the tide is just beginning to come in. Do you think I can stop it?"

The courtiers looked at each other. They knew, but they did not dare to give the answer in their minds.

"O yes, your majesty," they replied. "Nothing would disobey your orders."

"Good," said King Canute. "Come with me." He rose from his chair and stood at the water's edge with his courtiers about him.

"O sea," he declared in a loud voice. "Stay where you are! I, Canute, ruler of the universe, command you to come no further!"

He paused, and a small wave rushed over his ankles.

Canute did not move. He raised his voice again.

"Go back, I say. How dare you disobey me! The land on which I stand is mine—you have no right to advance upon it. Go back!"

As if in answer, the sea came on with greater force. A large wave splashed over the king and his courtiers, wetting them to the waist. Still they stood their ground. At last, when a huge breaker swept away the chair and threatened to drown the men, the courtiers ran, retreating to drier and safer land.

"You see," laughed Canute, "how little I am obeyed. Now," he added in a more serious tone, "you see that there is only one Lord over land and water, the Lord of the universe. It is to Him and to Him alone you should offer your praise."

Slowly the king and his courtiers walked back into the town. There, in front of them all, Canute took off his crown and hung it in the church. And there, in Southampton, is a bronze tablet which reads: "On this spot, in the year 1032, King Canute rebuked his courtiers."

RICHARD LION-HEART

...Saved by a Song

ICHARD the First was one of the greatest English
kings although he spent little time in England. He
was also Duke of Aquitaine and Normandy, and
wars in Europe as well as the Crusades in the Holy
Land kept him abroad during most of his reign in
the twelfth century. He was in the forefront of
every battle he fought. When he wielded his huge battle-axe none
could withstand him. So fearless was he that he was known not
merely as King Richard the Mighty but as Richard Lion-Heart.
Enemies fled when he charged upon them shouting his battle-cry,
"God be with us!"

Richard had gone on the Third Crusade against the Saracens,
hoping to drive them out of Jerusalem so that Christians could visit
the holy places in safety. He had been aided by two other European
kings, but he quarreled with his allies and grew to respect his
enemies more than his friends. Saladin, king of the Saracens, returned his respect and welcomed Richard as his guest. After mutual
acts of courtesy and expressions of good will, a three year truce was
proposed.

"We of the east believe greatly in the number three," said Saladin.
"It is a powerful number. Man is a threefold creature made of body,
soul, and spirit, and the enemies of man are three: the world, the
flesh, and the devil. Do you not believe so, you of the north?"

"It is so," replied Richard. "The Greeks taught us that man's life
depends on the three fates, that nature is divided into three king-
doms—animal, vegetable, and mineral—and that there are three
prime colors: red, yellow, and blue."

175

"That being true," said Saladin, "let us make our truce really binding. Let it be for three years, three months, three days, and three hours. And let us take an oath that nothing shall break such a truce."

The two leaders swore to keep the peace for that length of time and, if they were still friends, for the rest of their lives. Then Richard withdrew his troops from the Holy Land. He set sail for England by way of Cyprus, but a gale blew his ships off their course and drove them to Italy. Worse weather occurred when he resumed the journey. Storms overwhelmed the fleet with waves like battering-rams, and knife-sharp winds tore the sails. After a gruelling week, the boats lost contact with each other. King Richard's ship was thrown against a rocky coast and destroyed; his men were drowned, and he himself barely managed to survive.

After wandering for weeks, he found himself in the land of one of his worst enemies, Duke Leopold of Austria. He was recognized at once and captured. The Duke of Austria shut him up in a dungeon and then asked a huge ransom for his release. When Henry, Emperor of Germany, heard of this, he compelled Leopold to give up his prize but, instead of freeing Richard, Henry imprisoned him in one of his own castles and demanded a still more staggering ransom. So that no one would know where the king of England was hidden and attempt to rescue him, he had him moved at various times from one secret stronghold to another.

Meanwhile, things were going badly in England where Richard's absence had caused much confusion. There were rumors that the demand for ransom was a deception to get money for the German emperor and that Richard was really dead. His brother John robbed the treasury and plotted to seize the throne; the country was in a state of turmoil and anxiety. No one thought of clarifying the situation by finding out whether Richard was alive or dead. No one except Blondel de Nesle.

Blondel was a minstrel, a poet who was also a singer. He had been a boon companion to Richard in his youth. Richard and Blondel had spent many hours together making up tunes, matching rhymes, and composing songs on any subject that came to mind. It was Blondel who asked Richard's minister permission to look for the king.

"But how do you expect to conduct so wild a hunt?" inquired the minister. "Where will you start?"

"I cannot tell you *how* until I begin," answered Blondel. "But I can tell you *where*. The demands for the ransom have come from Germany, so Germany is the most likely place to start."

"How many men will you require?" asked the minister.

"None," said Blondel. "I will go alone."

"You will, I hope, be well armed. What weapons will you need?"

"One weapon only," said Blondel, "if you can call it that. I will take along my little hand harp. It will be all I need."

For three months Blondel wandered up and down Germany. He played his harp and sang his songs in taverns, inns, courtyards, and castles. He was always welcome, for people in every land delight to hear songs of war and wooing, of gallant deeds and lovely ladies, especially when they are sung as beautifully as Blondel sang them. He was offered large sums of money to remain in many a palace; he heard much gossip and was told many things in confidence. But never a word did he hear about King Richard.

One evening in autumn he came to an unusually large castle in the middle of a wild forest. It had a grim look, dark and desolate. Two equally grim guards stood in front of the drawbridge.

"Keep back," one of them said. "We make short work of spies."

"I am no spy," said Blondel. "I am a minstrel. I go from place to place to entertain lords and ladies. I am sure those inside would like to hear me."

"There is no one inside who cares for merrymaking," said the other guard. "Your eyes must be poor if you think this is a place for entertainment. It is not so much a castle as a prison."

"Indeed?" said Blondel. "I would not have suspected it."

"Yes," said the first guard, a note of pride coming into his voice. "It is one of the strongest prisons in Europe and one of the least known. And the curious part is this: it houses only one prisoner."

"And who might that be?" Blondel asked eagerly. "Who has an entire prison to himself?"

"That we can't tell you," replied the second guard. "In fact, we ourselves don't know. All we know is that he must be someone very important, someone who has to be watched very carefully."

"Well," said Blondel. "That is very interesting. But, after all, it has nothing to do with me. If I cannot get a welcome here I will try elsewhere. Before I go, perhaps you would like to hear a song."

"Go ahead," said the first guard. "A song never hurt anyone."

"Nor helped them, either," added the second. "But go ahead."

Blondel tuned his harp and began:

> My lady sits within her bower;
> She sings "alas" right dolefully:
> She lingers hour after hour
> For her true lord. But where is he?

Blondel paused. It was a song that he and King Richard had made up and sung together years ago. It had a new meaning now.

Then another voice was added to his, completing the second stanza:

> O tell my lady that the fates
> Have kept her lord away from men;
> But patiently her lover waits
> The day he can come home again.

The guards were startled to hear the second voice. They did not guess the meaning concealed in the song, but they were angry with themselves for having let the minstrel linger.

"That's enough!" shouted the guards. "On your way!"

Blondel went. But he had found what he had been seeking. He knew whose voice had answered him, and the captured king knew who had given him the message. He also knew that Blondel had discovered where he had been hidden. He did not have to wait long to be freed.

Three months later his release was accomplished and he was brought back to England. More powerful than ever, King Richard restored his country to peace.

ROBIN HOOD

...*And His Merry Men*

OBIN HOOD was an outlaw. There was no question about it. It was said in his behalf that he took from the rich to give to the poor. But he was, nevertheless, a wrongdoer, a rascal, a scamp, a ne'er-do-well, a breaker of the king's law. Most of all, he was a happy-go-lucky adventurer. He and his band of merry men made Sherwood Forest ring with their gladness, their games, and their gleeful songs.

It had come about in this way. While King Richard was fighting abroad for England, his brother John was misruling the country. John made cruel laws and let dishonest officers administer them; he seized property and caused thousands to suffer. Even the most loyal Englishmen complained of unjust hardships. One of these, the chief gamekeeper of Sherwood Forest, was not afraid to speak against the greedy king and especially against his henchman, the sheriff of Nottingham. For daring to tell the truth he was accused of treason, clapped into prison and, after weeks of torture, hanged. His wife died of the shock. His only son, Rob, was left to grow up in the wild woods by himself.

At eighteen, skilled in woodcraft and expert with bow and arrow, Rob determined to make his own way in the world. He had heard of a shooting match at Nottingham where the sheriff had offered a prize for the best archer. Polishing his bow made of stout yew wood and feathering his finest arrows, Rob set out for Nottingham. On the way through Sherwood Forest he came upon a group of rough-looking fellows at their midday meal.

"Look," said one of them, "a trespasser. And where, my lad, do you think you're going with your little toy bow and arrow?"

Robin knew he was being mocked, but he answered quietly.

"I'm going to the shooting-match at Nottingham, and I hope to win the prize."

"Oho!" laughed the first speaker. "A prize indeed! I doubt that you could hit a tree at a distance of twenty feet."

Rob bit his lips before he replied.

"I have only six shillings," he said, "but I'll wager that I can hit—do you see him?—the leader of the deer herd standing near the brook two hundred yards from here."

"What a boy! And what a boast!" jeered the man. "Soon you'll be mixing ale with your milk! I'll accept your wager. Let's see if you can draw a bow-string as well as an apron-string!"

Rob raised his yew bow, fitted an arrow, drew it close to his ear, and let it fly. It sang, and the leading deer fell.

"Now give me the six shillings," he said.

"Give you nothing!" snarled the man. "I said you were a trespasser. You are also a criminal. You've just killed one of the king's deer, and for that you should be put in prison. Here," he cried to the others, "lay hold of him."

Rob remembered what had happened to his parents—possibly these men were the very ones who had kidnapped his father for the sheriff—and he ran down the forest path. The man was furious.

"You won't get to Nottingham that way!" he shouted. "You won't get there at all——this will stop you!" He aimed an arrow at Rob.

Fortunately the man had been drinking and the shot whistled over lad's head. Before he could send a second arrow, Rob drew his own bow, and the man dropped to the ground. When the others went to raise him he had stopped breathing. Rob dashed through a trackless glade and disappeared.

That is how Rob became an outlaw. He hid himself in the forest and, exploring it from one end to the other, he found others who had been wronged, cheated, or accused of things they had never done. Some had broken the law—some had killed deer to save themselves from starving, some had been forced to steal in order to pay heavy debts—but most of them had been turned out of their homes or had run away from their landlords. Rob made friends with these homeless ones, brought them together and, within a year, had gathered about him almost a hundred men. They formed a small but wonderfully united army. They became excellent archers and swordsmen; and, so that their clothing might blend with the forest colors and make them almost invisible, they dressed

in Sherwood green. They lived on what they could find, catch, or kill. Since the woodland was rich with fruit and game, they lived very well. The country folk around were not afraid of them. On the contrary, Rob's men were much admired for they helped the poor when they were in need and kept many a family out of the clutches of the grasping sheriff. Because Rob wore a hood that fell over his shoulders, he was called "Rob-in-the-hood," soon shortened to Robin Hood, a name by which he became known throughout the countryside.

One spring morning, Robin Hood said to his men, "I feel something stirring in the air. It's the season for adventure, and I'm going looking for it. Do what you like until I return. If I need you I will blow three blasts on my horn, a signal for you to come quickly wherever you are."

Wandering with a light heart he came to a small stream. Instead of a bridge, it was spanned by a rough log. As Robin put his foot on the log, a tall man about his own age started to cross from the other side.

"Back!" said Robin. "Give way to the better man."

"I see no better man," said the stranger, "unless I look at myself in the stream. Then I see a man who could get the better of any other man, here or anywhere else."

Robin drew a dagger from his side.

"Surely," said the stranger, "you would not kill an unarmed man. I have nothing but a wooden staff to protect me. Take up a piece of wood for a staff, then let us see who is truly the better man."

Robin cut a branch from an oak tree and, while he trimmed it, eyed the stranger who stood whistling at his ease. Robin was tall, but the stranger was taller, almost seven feet in height and his shoulders were even broader than Robin's. "Here," said Robin to himself, "is a lusty adventure, a true test of skill and strength."

Then, in a loud voice, he cried "Have at you!" and struck the first blow.

It was aimed at the stranger's head, but it was stopped by the stranger's staff. It glanced off his shoulder while he, in turn, swung at Robin, who parried the stroke with his oak branch. For a while it was blow after blow, a thwacking and a thudding that landed on ribs and elbows, but neither man would give way to the other. Both stood balancing themselves on the log until the stranger delivered so mighty a thrust that Robin was toppled into the stream.

"Ha!" laughed the stranger. "You may not be the better man, but you certainly are the wetter one!"

Robin spluttered but he, too, could not help laughing. The stranger held out a hand and brought Robin to his feet. "For my bruises, I should give you the beating you deserve," he chuckled.

"Hold your hand," said Robin. "A stout fellow such as you would not hurt a dripping man who has no foothold on the slippery ground." Then he blew three blasts on his horn.

Before the echoes had died twenty men sprang out of the trees.

"Shall we strip him of his clothes?" they cried. "Or shall we string him up?"

"Don't touch him," said Robin. "He is a hardy fellow; there isn't a man between here and London who could do what he has done to me."

"And you are a brave one," said the stranger. "You give and take punishment like one of the heroes of old."

"A truce to compliments," said Robin. "You see some of my men here. There are many more in the greenwood waiting. We live by our skill with the bow and also by our wits. We waylay none but puffed-up lords carrying well-filled purses and fat merchants with stuffed money-bags. When we get together there is a feast of the sweetest venison you ever tasted washed down with good nut-brown ale. Ours is a merry band. Will you join it?"

"I'm not sure," said the stranger. "If you have no more skill with a bow than you showed with that oak branch, I would not put my trust in you."

Robin's men were angered; they were about to lay hands on the stranger when Robin held them back.

"Let us see how good a marksman he may be," he said quietly. "Cut a small round piece of white birch bark and set it up on that pine tree some eighty yards away."

When it was done, he handed his bow to the stranger. The tall man twanged the string a moment, chose a smooth feathered arrow and sent it straight to the mark. It hit the white target in the very center.

"A good shot," said Robin. "I can't surpass that, but perhaps I can spoil it."

The next second Robin's arrow flew to the mark. His aim was so sure and the flight so swift that his arrow hit the stranger's shaft and split it in two.

"I bow to my master," said the stranger. "When can I join your band?"

"As soon as you have told us what they call you," said Robin.

"My name is John Little."

"Your name *was* John Little," said Robin, looking at the huge fellow. "The joke is too good to miss. From now on it will be Little John."

Little John it became. He was baptized with a pot of ale and soon was Robin's second in command. It was Little John who was chosen by Robin for an especially dangerous mission.

"The sheriff of Nottingham has put a price of one hundred silver pounds upon my head," Robin told Little John. "He has sworn to capture me and my merry men. But he fears to come into Sherwood Forest, for we know all the ins and outs of the woods, while they can fight only in the open. What he hopes is to snare us into town for some tournament or shooting-match. Meanwhile, he has posted groups of his men along the edge of the forest. They lie in wait for any of us who might stray into the highways. I would like to know where and how many they are."

"I am your man," said Little John. "I will disguise myself as a pilgrim, with a monk's gown and a cowl over my head. Then I can take to the open road and mingle with anyone I chance to meet."

Robin wished him godspeed and Little John set out toward Nottingham. Crossing the highway he came to an inn, The Blue Boar. A dozen men sat under a swinging sign eating a stew and drinking from pewter tankards. Little John knew they were the sheriff of Nottingham's men; it was easy to get into conversation with them. Soon they were talking about themselves.

"Yes, brother," said one of them, "we are the sheriff's men—at least we are a few of his force. There are more than a hundred of us at different places in the neighborhood, and we will patrol these parts until we get the green-clad villain they call Robin Hood. But tell me, brother, where are you going?"

"I am making a pilgrimage to Canterbury," replied Little John, tossing a scrap of meat to a dog that brushed against him. The dog begged for more.

"It's a long way," said the man. "Do you go on foot?"

"That is part of my penance," said Little John. What he did not notice, when the dog put its paw on his knee, was that his robe had been raised a few inches. The man noticed it.

"What kind of friar is this who wears Sherwood green under his robe!" he cried and leaped to his feet. "This is a scoundrel——he can be no other than one of Robin Hood's men. Here!" he cried to the others. "Hold this fellow. He is a thief, a spy sent by that lord of thieves, Robin Hood! Don't let him get away!"

Little John struggled, but it was useless. His robe encumbered him; he could not even reach the dagger he had concealed in his shoe. They bound his hands and feet and dragged him to a cart, treating him roughly all the way to Nottingham.

The innkeeper of The Blue Boar happened to be a cousin of Will Scarlett, one of Robin Hood's best men. He slipped away and got word to his cousin the same day. By the time Little John had arrived in Nottingham, Robin Hood knew all the details. Three bugle blasts called his men together.

"They have taken Little John," he told them. "The sheriff is overjoyed. He has given his men a large reward and has promised the townspeople a great show. He says he will put Little John to death tomorrow, and will leave his body hanging on the gallows as a warning to all other outlaws. Time is short. We go to Nottingham immediately, but we go in the clothing of tradesmen with bags of merchandise. Let us be sure that those bags contain something sharper than laces and looking glasses. Go now and prepare. Be ready to leave by midnight."

It was a chill morning when they brought Little John to the square in the center of Nottingham. Stands had been put up to make a show of the hanging, and crowds had been gathering since dawn. Flags were flying and a bagpipe player circled among the throng. At nine o'clock the sheriff appeared in a glistening coat of mail, accompanied by a troop of men-at-arms. Drums rolled and a cart rumbled into the square carrying the battered prisoner. One eye was blackened, his hair was matted, his face was streaked with dried blood. He raised his head and addressed the sheriff.

"A boon," said Little John.

"What right has a thief to ask favor?" said the sheriff.

"It is a wounded man who speaks," said Little John. "A wounded man who asks the loan of a sword. You are fifty to one, but a wounded man should have the right to fight his way out, if he can."

"Ask no favors of me," sneered the sheriff. "Ask your friends. See if any here will favor you."

Little John looked. He saw people who regarded him with pity, and people who looked unhappy at what was to come, but none offered any hope. Then he noticed a merchant whose face seemed familiar and, as he looked again, the merchant winked broadly at him. A few feet away another merchant raised his hand, and Little John caught the glitter of sunlight on steel. Those in the crowd who did not have seats pressed closer.

"Stand back!" called the sheriff. "We will not permit any jostling. This will be an orderly hanging."

But the jostling continued. A couple of merchants pushed between the men-at-arms and the soldiers pushed back.

"I said stand back!" cried the sheriff angrily.

"Stand back yourself!" came a ringing voice. It was the voice of Will Scarlett who brought his short sword down on the head of the nearest man-at-arms. There was confusion and an uproar. The men-at-arms had no time to act; they were seized from behind, knocked about, and tossed aside. While Will Scarlett blocked the way of the

sheriff, Robin Hood sprang into the cart and cut the cords that
bound Little John. The sympathetic crowd surged around the
sheriff's men, making it impossible for them to use their weapons.
The sheriff himself tried to rally his men, but they were in panic.
They fled when an arrow struck their leader a glancing blow, and
the sheriff was left alone to face Robin Hood.

"You deserve to die," said Robin. "But I am in no mood for revenge. Besides, I do not kill cowards. Go home and nurse your
wound. Next time the arrow will go deeper."

Robin Hood and his men spurred their horses toward the city
gates. The crowd divided to let them pass, as they rode down the
streets, over the highway, and into the protective depth of Sherwood
Forest.

Many were the further adventures of Robin Hood. There was the
time when he saved a poor widow's three blameless sons from the
sheriff's gallows; the time he disguised himself as a harper and won
back Allen-a-Dale's sweetheart who was being forced to become
the bride of a rich old man; the time he rescued from poverty an
honorable knight whose entire property had been stolen from him;
and the time a traveling tinker showed so much mettle that he was
made a member of the band. But the greatest adventure of all was
the surprise that happened right in Sherwood Forest.

Richard Lion-Heart had come home from the Crusades and was
making a triumphal progress through the land. Never had there
been so royal a homecoming. Banners and trumpets hailed his entry
into every town; streets were lined with ribbons and flowers; men,
women, and children cheered as he went by. And everywhere he
went he heard tales of Robin Hood. Some praised the outlaw's gallant deeds; others condemned him as a wicked scoundrel. "I must
learn more about this man," said the king to himself.

One day, while Robin Hood and his men were tanning a deer's
hide, a tall stranger appeared before them. He was dressed in the
Order of the Black Friars and he said he had lost his way.

"I am looking to find Newstead Abbey," he told Robin. "But I
have traveled far and am footsore. Perhaps you could let me rest
here a while. Besides, the dust of the road is in my throat, and I
would give a pound for a good thirst-quenching drink."

"That is the best bargain I have heard in a long time," said
Robin. "You shall not only drink but eat with us. We're just about
ready to dine. Our fare is fairly simple, but I think you will find it
plentiful."

It was, in every sense, a feast fit for a king. There was spiced hare, stuffed roast pheasant, and a lordly haunch of venison, accompanied by liberal flagons of cream ale. At the end of the meal, Robin proposed a toast.

"A health to our newly-returned king, and a curse upon his enemies."

The friar put down his tankard of ale. "Aren't you calling down a curse upon yourself?" he said. "You're one of the king's enemies, aren't you?"

Robin sprang to his feet. "You are lucky to be my guest," he said. "Otherwise I would slit your throat for saying that. No one can call me an enemy of King Richard the lion-hearted."

"But," continued the friar without a trace of fear, "you are an outlaw, a lawbreaker with a price on your head."

"It's true we break the law," said Robin. "But it is not the king's law. It is the rule of the king's unworthy creatures, his heartless minions, that we oppose. We are more loyal to King Richard than most people—even than you. While you friars and priests sleep snugly in your abbeys, we risk our freedom, preparing for the day when King Richard will need us. When that time comes we stand ready to give our lives for him."

The friar laughed. "I am sure the king would be glad to hear that," he said. "He would be fortunate to have so faithful a body-guard—and, from what I can see, such an efficient one. But we have talked enough about kings and the law. Can't we end the meal with something livelier? It is told that you are all wonderful archers. Would you care to entertain a stranger with a show of your skill?"

"Right gladly," said Robin. "Two of my men, Little John and Will Scarlett, will set up the marks."

Will Scarlett made a wreath of leaves and wild flowers, and Little John nailed it to a tree more than two hundred yards from where Robin and the friar were standing.

"Each of my men will shoot three arrows through the center of that circle," said Robin. "If anyone misses by even a single arrow he shall receive a stout blow from my fist."

"This promises to be good sport," said the friar. "And what happens if *you* should miss the mark?"

"I am no boaster," said Robin, "but I never miss."

One after the other Robin's men shot at the leafy mark. Some of their arrows hit the very center; some came near the edge of the circle, but none missed it. Soon the target was so crowded that a new wreath had to be put up.

Robin was the last to shoot. His first two arrows crowded each other in the center of the wreath but, as he loosed the third arrow, a large bird flew close to his head, and, while he tried to brush it off, the arrow went wide of the mark.

All the men laughed loudly, the friar loudest of all. Robin laughed with them, though he said, "That arrow must have had a poor feather in it. Still, I must abide by my own rule. Since I am king of the forest and none of my subjects may raise a hand against their king, I will accept the blow only from the friar, if he would be gracious enough to bestow the punishment."

"That I will do gladly," said the friar, and dealt Robin so mighty a buffet that he fell as though struck down by a thunderbolt.

"Never would I have believed," said Robin rubbing his head, "that any friar could deliver such a clout. Now," he added as he got to his feet, "see if you can withstand this counterblow." And he gave the friar as staggering a cuff as he had received. The friar, thrown backward, fell sprawling among the leaves.

At that moment a group of the king's cavalry crashed into the glade.

"Your majesty!" the leader began in amazement. Then, catching sight of Robin's bared arm, he cried "Sacrilege! You have struck the king! For that you will die! Seize him!"

"Nay," said the friar, removing his robe and revealing the royal armor underneath. "Let him be. It was a fair exchange, an exchange of courtesies between the king of the forest and the king of the country. These men are to be pardoned. They are no longer outlaws; they shall enter my employ as royal rangers, gamekeepers, caretakers of the king's woodlands. As for you, Robin, you lawless rogue, you will break no more laws, for you shall be part of my personal service and uphold the law of the land. You will have to learn to bend the knee, but not as a menial. You used to rob the rich, now you will feel what it is like to be one of the robbed. Bend your knee, for I shall make you Earl of Huntingdon."

So Robin Hood's adventures had the happiest of endings. Robin became one of King Richard's favorites. He followed him to foreign wars and returned to England as the most faithful of the king's subjects. The king never tired of his company, and the ballad-singers never stopped singing of Robin Hood and his merry men, his daring and all his gallant deeds.

KING JOHN AND THE ABBOT

... *The Three Questions*

 PON the death of Richard Lion-Heart, his younger brother, John, became king. King John lived not only richly and royally but, even for a king, extravagantly. He had many castles, and each of them outshone the other with lordly towers, marble floors, bronze doors, and tapestries that made the walls sing with color. He dressed his servants in cloth of gold; he presented his guests with garments of heavy silk, jewelled rings, and coats of precious furs. He served the most sumptuous meals on plates of pure silver. No one in the kingdom lived as well as its king —no one except the Abbot of Canterbury.

For a while King John permitted the abbot to rival him in luxury. Finally he could control his jealousy no longer. He summoned the abbot.

"Father Abbot," he began quietly, "I hear that you have a hundred knights to wait on you every day. I hear that you furnish them with velvet coats and gold chains. In short, I hear that you keep a far better household than I do. This, you know, is treason."

"Your Majesty," replied the abbot, "I would be the last man in your kingdom to have even the smallest thought of disloyalty. As to treason—I spend only what is my own. It is true that I entertain my guests in fair style; but that does credit to the abbey and, in a broad sense, to England."

"Yes, yes, I knew you would say something of the sort," said King John, beginning to lose his temper. "Surely you know that all property in England belongs to the crown. But I didn't bring you here to argue with you. I brought you here to tell you that you are

191

192 KING JOHN AND THE ABBOT

guilty of treason, that you deserve to be executed, and that all your possessions should be turned over to me."

"Your Majesty" cried the abbot. "I cannot believe——"

"Keep your belief for your sermons," angrily interrupted the king. "However," he resumed, calming himself, "as everyone knows, I am a merciful monarch. I will spare your life as well as your property if you can convince me of your wisdom and answer three questions."

"I shall try, your Majesty," said the abbot. "What are the three questions?"

"First," said King John, "as I sit here with this crown of gold on my head, you must tell me to the day how long I shall live. Second, you must tell me how long it will take me to ride around the entire world. Third, you must tell me what I am thinking."

"But, your Majesty——" began the abbot.

"No more buts," snapped the king. "I will give you seven days to decide on your answers. If you are not here with the right answers exactly one week from today, your life and lands and all the things you possess will be forfeit to me."

Sadly the abbot rode away. He went to Oxford, hoping some scholar at one of the great colleges there could supply the answers. When none could help, he rode to Cambridge; but the learned men there were no wiser. Shaking his head—a head that would, alas, soon be severed from his shoulders—he turned toward home. He had wasted four days; there were only three days left.

As he neared his abbey he met a shepherd. "Welcome back, master," said the shepherd. "What news do you bring from court and King John?"

"Bad news," replied the abbot. "Bad news indeed. I have only three days to live unless I answer three questions."

"Surely that should not be hard for you," said the shepherd. "What are the questions?"

When the doleful abbot told him what they were, the shepherd grinned. "Cheer up, master. Do not despair. Sometimes a fool may teach a wise man something. Let me, the fool, go to London. Lend me some of your servants, a few of your knights, your horse, and your gown. Begging your pardon, but it has often been said that my features resemble yours and, with a hood over my head, it would be hard to tell the difference between us. Let me do what I suggest ——perhaps this fool can fool the king."

"But the questions?" said the abbot. "What will you do when you stand in front of King John?"

"I think I know a way to satisfy him—and save you, too," said the shepherd.

The next day the shepherd, accompanied by a splendid retinue, rode into London. Dressed like the abbot, he carried the gold staff and other symbols of the abbot's churchly office.

"Welcome, Sir Abbot," said King John. "You are prompt; you are even two days ahead of time. That is good. However, prompt as you are, I trust you haven't forgotten our bargain. You must answer my three questions in order to save your life and your property. Are you ready?"

"I am ready, your Majesty," said the disguised shepherd.

"First, as I sit here with this crown of gold on my head, tell me to the day how long I shall live."

"That's easy, your Majesty," replied the shepherd. "You will live until you die, not one day longer and not one hour less."

The king laughed. "A very clever answer. Your wit has saved you this time. Now for the second question. How long will it take me to ride around the entire world?"

"That, your Majesty, is even easier. If at sunrise you get up and ride with the sun, and continue to ride with it until it rises again the next morning, you will have ridden around the entire world in exactly twenty-four hours."

King John laughed still more heartily. "I didn't think it could be done so easily," he said. "You are as wise as you are witty. Now for the last and hardest question. Tell me what I am thinking."

This time it was the shepherd who laughed. "That's the easiest of all," he said. "You are thinking I am the Abbot of Canterbury, but I am only a poor foolish shepherd dressed in his robes. And I have come here to ask pardon for him."

For a moment the king frowned. Then he chuckled. Then he roared with laughter until he had to hold his sides.

"You rogue!" he cried. "I ought to have you hanged! Instead I will make you Lord Abbot of Canterbury in place of the one who is hiding there."

"Thank you, your Majesty," said the shepherd, snatching off the abbot's cap and bowing deeply. "But that's impossible. I can neither read nor write."

"In that case," smiled the king, "I will see that you get a reward, four pieces of silver every week. The joke was worth it. And when you get home, you can tell the abbot that, thanks to your cleverness, he has a pardon from King John. Tell him I wish him to live long— but not *quite* so well."

KING JOHN AND THE MAGNA CARTA

...What Happened at Runnymede

 VER since childhood King John had been selfish, greedy, and jealous. In the first years of his rule he had a sense of fair play, even—as in his dealings with the Abbot of Canterbury—some sense of humor. However, as his power grew, his sense of fairness and occasional playfulness vanished. He became mean, violent and vicious.

Actually he was not the rightful king of England; his nephew, Prince Arthur, should have been on the throne. Using the excuse that Arthur was too young to rule, John had him sent to France, a large part of which was under the domination of England. Arthur eventually asserted himself and headed an army, but he was defeated and captured. Shakespeare's *King John* contains a heart-rending scene in which, commanded by the king, Hubert, the prince's keeper, comes to put out Arthur's eyes and is so moved by the youth's goodness and innocence that he cannot carry out the order. Though Arthur had been spared by Hubert, King John saw to it that his nephew did not live much longer. His broken body was found at the foot of the castle. One report had it that Arthur tried to escape and had jumped from a high tower. Another told of a masked figure who claimed he had come to rescue the prince and, taking Arthur to a dark corner, stabbed him to death. The figure, they said, was that of his uncle.

The king's nobles, his knights and barons, had always distrusted John. They had whispered about his cruelties for some time. Now they were bitterly outspoken.

"There is no sure foundation set on split blood," said one of them.

"He has killed and robbed for years," said another. "After he has

196   KING JOHN AND THE MAGNA CARTA

seized property to which he has no right, he wastes it. No wonder men call him John Lackland instead of King John."

"How much longer will we submit to the rule of such a villain!" angrily cried a third baron. "There must be some way to punish a robbing tyrant who doesn't even stop at murder!"

"We need not return villainy for villainy," added a milder voice. "We are powerful enough to make demands and, what is more, to see that they are granted."

The last speaker was Stephen Langton, Archbishop of Canterbury. He had won the love as well as the respect of all who knew him. Until this moment he had kept out of political affairs, but now he took the lead in the discussions.

"It is time for us to show that we are free men, not vassals of an evil monarch. We must not plead for promises that we know will be broken. We must demand—and have those demands put in writing. We must go further. We must make him accept and sign those demands. Even this king must abide by his signature."

Unaccustomed to such boldness, some of the barons drew back; most of them clustered about Langton.

"How shall we go about it?" they asked.

"First swear that we will act together—and stay together. Swear that we will not rest until the king signs a guarantee of human rights. Swear that we will go to war, if necessary, for those rights."

"But," objected one of the barons, "that is treason."

"Better treason," said Langton, "than slavery."

Moved by his eloquence and convinced by his argument, the barons swore to press their claims upon the king. Then, with their troops, they marched on London. King John received them and tried to persuade them that they were doing a foolish thing.

"A king rules by divine right," he protested. "Surely you do not expect me to sign away such a right."

When he saw that he could not make them change their minds, he postponed the decision.

"It is a monstrous thing you are proposing," he said. "I will have to think about it. This is the Christmas season, no time for such matters. Come back at Easter and we will talk about it again."

The barons departed reluctantly, for they knew they were being put off. When Easter came, King John tried to put them off again. This time, however, they came with a huge army gathered from all parts of the kingdom. The king fumed and fretted and managed to delay things a little, but decided not to stand against the barons

when he learned that only seven knights could be counted on to side with him.

It was a sunny day in June, in the year 1215, when the two groups met at the green field of Runnymede on the river Thames. The king's men were drawn up on one side of the river, Langton's men on the other. Crossing to a little island in midstream, Langton presented the Magna Carta, or Great Charter. It contained thirty-seven parts, and King John sat stony-faced while it was read to him line by line. It was more than a document. It was not only a token of justice for the knights and barons but also for all people against abuses by those high in power. It promised that no man would be imprisoned without a fair trial, that property would be respected, that there would be free elections, and that no one would be oppressed or denied his rights.

Forced to sign the Magna Carta, King John tried to break its firm foundation. When the barons made this impossible, he stormed and raved. It is said that he beat his fists against the wall, threw himself on the floor, and foamed at the mouth with speechless fury. He could not rest. He shrieked, "within me is a hell!" Unable to regain his power he fell into a raging fever and, in a last outburst of anger, died.

Because he was a king, he was given a royal funeral, but no one mourned his death. His pride and cruelty had cost him every friend he might have had.

ROBERT THE BRUCE

...What a Spider Taught a King

OR years Scotland and England had been bitter enemies. Nevertheless, in the thirteenth century when the Scottish leaders were fighting among themselves about which one of them was entitled to be king, the rival claimants appealed to Edward I of England to decide who should wear the crown. Edward's decision was scarcely what they expected.

"The only person worthy to be your king must have all the qualities of kingship," he said. "Therefore I appoint myself king of Scotland as well as England."

Edward sent an army across the border and carried off to England not only the Scottish crown and all the royal regalia but also the sacred Stone of Scone on which the kings of Scotland had always been crowned and placed it in Westminster Abbey, where it still rests. He thought this outrage would break the last resistance of the Scots, but he underestimated their proud spirit.

The Scots refused to be governed by anyone except themselves. They rebelled and went to battle under the command of Sir William Wallace. When Wallace was beaten, they chose Robert Bruce as their leader, had him secretly crowned king, at Scone, and defied the English. Their defiance was greater than their military resources, however. An invading English army overwhelmed them and drove them into hiding.

For almost a year the Scottish defenders kept to themselves in scattered groups. They stayed in the woods, living on eels and salmon that swam in the streams and, like Robin Hood and his followers, on the deer that roamed the forest. They did not enjoy their woodland respite long. The English attacked with fresh troops,

forced them out, and scattered the remnants of the Scottish army.
Badly wounded, Bruce managed to escape.

Escape was difficult, for the English had captured one of Bruce's
best bloodhounds and were hunting him down with it. Bruce threw
off his coat, dodged among the trees and crouched under bushes
that had a strong fragrance, but he could not throw the hound off
his scent. He knew the dog, and knew by its joyous barking that the
dog had recognized his footsteps, was hot on the trail, and would
soon catch up with him. Bruce ran on blindly, not daring to stop or
look back. Exhausted, he was about to fall to the ground when he
found himself at the edge of a broad brook. He plunged into the
water, knowing that the dog would follow his scent to this point
and that his pursuers would expect him to cross the stream and
continue his flight on the other side. After the men had crossed the
stream, they stood puzzled. The dog could find no scent of his master
on the other bank, and so, after thrashing about for a while, the
English soldiers gave up their search.

Bruce had fooled them. Instead of crossing the stream, he had waded along the edge of the brook for quite a ways and then, seeing a low branch hanging near the water, had seized it, climbed from one bough to another, and lay hidden in the tree all the time his enemies were hunting for him.

After a while Bruce made his way carefully out of the woods and into the hills where he found a safe refuge among the steep crags and wild glens of the uplands. He spent most of the winter months in a broken-down hovel, keeping himself alive on a bag of old potatoes that had been left there, on acorns and nuts, and an occasional rabbit that he was lucky to catch.

One cold gray afternoon he was sitting hunched up, cheerless and almost hopeless, gazing outdoors at the dreary landscape. As he looked, he noticed a spider trying to weave a web in the corner of the window. The creature was having a hard time of it. The pane was cracked and every time the spider would fasten a thin strand to the edge of wood, a draft would blow the thread down. Six times the insect tried to hold the bit of spun silk in place, and six times it failed.

"I might be that spider," Bruce thought. "I, too, have failed. Like those threads, my lines have been broken and blown away. They are too frail; they will not hold for a downhearted man."

But the spider had not lost heart. Once more it tried. Bruce watched as it spun another thread and, seemingly, a stronger one. This time it held.

"You brave thing!" Bruce exclaimed. "You have shown me that there is always one more time—a time for one more attempt and, with persistence, a winning one!"

Bruce left the hovel and went to look for his scattered troops with new hope and renewed courage. He found them here and there, gathered them together, and by spring he had an army that was tougher than ever. The Scots fought stubbornly, battle after battle. Their lines held, increasing in strength until the final triumph when, at Bannockburn, although facing an army far superior in numbers, they drove the English out of Scotland.

Ever since then no one by the name of Bruce has ever killed a spider. At least so they say.

DICK WHITTINGTON

...*Who Owed Everything to a Cat*

HINGS were going badly in England during the fourteenth century. The Hundred Years' War had begun and countless Englishmen died in foreign lands. Families lost fathers, and many homes were left without enough food to keep the widows and orphans alive.

The Whittington family was one of those hardest hit. The father had been killed in France and the grieving mother died soon afterward. Their young son, Dick, was left alone in the world. The boy was too young to take care of the farm which had supported them and soon it was nothing but overgrown weeds. The cattle were seized by the soldiers and the barns were falling down. Dick could find no work in the village and, even if he had not been too proud to accept charity, there was no one to whom he could turn. He made up his mind to try to find work in the city and started out for London.

London was a long way from his village and Dick trudged on for miles. Although many carts passed him, none offered a lift. Finally a hay wagon stopped and the driver, a fat, jolly fellow, invited Dick to sit beside him.

"Where are you bound for, my lad?" the driver asked.

"London, sir," said Dick. "And what kind of a place is it, if you know?"

"Well, now," said the driver, "that's where I'm going, and I know London very well indeed. I've been there many times. It's a city of great churches and noble houses and fine ladies and gentlemen." He could not help teasing the boy a little. "You'll be sure to make your fortune there. Everyone in London is rich. Why, the streets are paved with gold."

Dick could hardly wait to reach the city. But, once there, his heart sank. There were great churches and noble houses, and he saw many fine ladies and gentlemen. But there was not a trace of gold lying around. Dick had thought all he needed to do was to scrape little pieces from the pavement and pocket the wealth. The streets, however, were filthy, and when he cleaned some of the dirt from the stones, there was not the slightest glitter underneath.

The well-dressed ladies and gentlemen were not what he expected either. When he asked about a place to sleep, the ladies turned their heads away from the dusty, ill-clad country boy, while the gentlemen ignored his question and told him sharply to get off the streets and go to work. The few pennies Dick had brought with him were soon gone and he was forced to sleep in alleys. Faint with hunger—for he would not beg food—and exhausted from days of walking looking for employment, he could hardly hold himself up. At last he crept into a doorway and, although it was still daylight, fell asleep.

Suddenly he was shaken and pulled to his feet by a towering, bad-tempered woman.

"Out! Out!" she cried. "Do you think Mr. Fitzwarren wants dirty little beggars sleeping at his door! If you're not gone in two minutes I'll throw a pail of dishwater over your head!"

She started to push Dick out with her broom——almost into the arms of Mr. Fitzwarren himself who appeared at that moment.

"What's this?" he inquired. "Cook, put down your broom! This boy looks ill and starved. Tell me, boy, when did you last eat?"

"I'm not sure, sir," said Dick. "I think it was three days ago."

"We must do something about that," said Mr. Fitzwarren. "Cook, take the boy to the kitchen. Clean him up and give him a bite of supper. Then send him to me."

After supper Dick told his story to Mr. Fitzwarren.

"Well, now," said the gentleman, "since you are looking for work, you can work here. There's plenty to do, especially in the kitchen. Just do what you're told, try not to get under the cook's heels, and try not to mind her tongue."

Dick thanked his benefactor, but it was not easy to follow his advice. The cook was a mean-spirited woman who did not like children. She took a special dislike to Dick. Although she had to do what her master told her, she made it as hard as possible for the boy. She had him do all the scullery work, kept him scouring pots and pans, polishing the silver and pewter, scrubbing the spit, and running errands until he almost dropped. At night it was all he could do to walk up to his attic room. He fell asleep almost before his head touched the straw pillow.

One wintry morning while Dick was cleaning the front steps he saw a shivering kitten crouched just where he had fallen asleep a few months before. The kitten did not run away but looked at him as though appealing for help. It was a thin little thing with smooth, silver-gray hair; it had amber-colored eyes and a tiny pink nose. Dick stooped to stroke it and it jumped into his arms. It whimpered for a moment, but then, as Dick rubbed its little head, it made a low rumbling sound, and Dick knew it was pleased.

"I'm going to keep you, if I can," said Dick. "Shall I call you Purry because of the way you purr? No, I think I've a better name for you. You've such a fine silky coat, I think I'll call you Furry. How does that suit you?"

"Merow," said the kitten.

"Good," said Dick. "I'm glad you like it. Furry you are, and Furry you shall be."

When the cook saw the kitten she was beside herself.

"It isn't enough to have to look out for you," she stormed at Dick, "to watch what you are doing—or *not* doing—to feed you and put up with your foolishness! But now you drag in a filthy animal for me to feed and clean up after! I won't have it! Out it goes!"

"Please, please, let me keep it," begged Dick. "Please! It's so tiny. I'll give it scraps of my own food and see that it's kept out of your way, and I'll clean up after it."

"Yes, cook, let him keep the little creature," said Mr. Fitzwarren from the doorway. "It might even get rid of the mice you tell me make their home in the pantry. Besides it may make a nice pet for Alice." (Mr. Fitzwarren's daughter Alice was just about Dick's age.)

So Furry remained. Dick always saved some of his milk for his growing tabby. She ate from his hand and, when he was through eating, she licked his plate. At night she would follow him to his cold garret and, lying on his chest, keep him warm. Although Furry looked soft and silky, she was a great huntress. She chased and fed on the toughest mice and was not afraid of the fiercest rats. She put on weight and, in less than three years, was the sleekest, finest, and most fearless cat in London. She allowed no one but Dick and Alice to stroke her head and rub her chest.

Dick was seventeen when he was called into Mr. Fitzwarren's office.

"One of my merchant ships is ready to sail," he told Dick. "It is my custom to let all my servants have some share in the venture. Besides the regular cargo, the ship will take things from our household to exchange for money or foreign merchandise. Some of the servants are sending trinkets, and others clothes to be sold. Is there anything you would like to sell?"

"I have nothing except Furry," said Dick. "And I would not want to part with her. Besides, who would want a cat?"

"Why, the captain of the ship would welcome a cat on board, particularly such a hunter as your Furry," said Mr. Fitzwarren. "He has often complained that the hold of his ship is overrun with pests. You would not have to sell your fine mouser, either. You could just rent her. I will ask the captain to give you six shillings for the loan of her, and to have her back in no more than five months."

Six shillings was not a great deal of money, but it was something, a step, six steps, toward the fortune that Dick never stopped dreaming about. Besides, he could not refuse Mr. Fitzwarren. Furry sailed, and Dick resigned himself to being without his pet.

For a while Dick went about his work, trying not to show how lonely he was. But he could not conceal his sadness. The cook made fun of him and was meaner than ever when he moped. Alice tried to comfort him, to play games and cheer him up by saying that the ship would be coming home soon. But the months dragged on and, when five months had passed and the ship did not return, Dick was downhearted.

One morning before dawn he decided to get away from London and go back to the farm and work in the country. He got as far as the outskirts of the city when he sat down on a stone—now known as the Whittington Stone—to rest. As he sat trying to make up his mind which road to take, the great bells of Bow Church began to ring. They played the same chime over and over and, as they played, they seemed to be saying something. It was as if the bells were speaking especially to him:

> Turn again—Dick Whittington—
> Turn again—and you will be—
> Three—three—three—
> Three times Lord Mayor of London.

"What nonsense!" Dick thought. "Still, that is what the bell did say, or seemed to say. Perhaps it is a promise or a warning of some kind. In any case, Lord Mayor or not, I think I should heed the voice of the bells. I am going to turn back to London, no matter what!"

Dick reached the house just before the cook came down to make breakfast. That same afternoon the captain of the ship arrived. He sat with Mr. Fitzwarren for quite a while. Then Dick was called in.

"Here," said the captain, "is your precious cat—and very precious she was, too."

"She still is—more than ever," cried Dick, as Furry, purring and miaowing in the same breath, sprang into his arms and licked his face.

"And here are your six shillings for the loan of her. And there's something more, said the captain. "It is in this black box which I brought back with me. Before you open it, I must tell you what happened.

"By the time we reached the Barbary Coast, your Furry had done wonders aboard ship. Never had the vessel been so free of rodents; never had any of my sailors made such a fuss over a cat. Even my first mate, who is a cat-hater, liked to pick her up and play with her. When we reached Morocco the brown-colored natives brought us a message from the king of the country, inviting us to dinner.

"Of course we took gifts and sold and exchanged many of the things we had with us. Then we sat down to dine. Dozens of silver platters and golden dishes were brought in. But as soon as the covers were taken off, a huge horde of rats and mice leaped upon the food, snapping morsels and carrying the larger pieces away. There was not much left for the company.

"'This is horrible,' I said to the king. 'Why do you allow it?'

"'It is something we cannot help,' he replied. 'Our cook has to prepare more than three times as much as we can eat in order to have something left for ourselves. We have tried to clear the palace of the greedy monsters, but there seems no way to get rid of them. And they not only devour our food, but attack us while we sleep. I cannot tell you how much I would give for a remedy.'

"'I think I have one,' I said. 'It's on board by ship. Shall I bring it?'

"'By all means,' the king answered. 'I am curious to see what it may be.'

"An hour later I brought Furry all bundled up into the palace. You should have watched the king's face when I let the cat out of the bag! If you had seen what that cat did then you would have changed her name from Furry to Fury! Never in my life did I see such furious pounces and savage, lightning-fast leaps. In half an hour twenty or more mice and rats lay dead at her feet. The rest were lucky to get to their holes. When the last of them had disappeared, Furry sat calmly cleaning her whiskers and washing her paws.

" 'What a marvellous creature!' cried the king. 'I must have her. Name your price.'

" 'Your Majesty,' I said, 'she is not for sale. She does not belong to me.'

"The king pleaded and begged for her. He promised to give me the cat's weight in solid gold; he offered rare silks and precious stones. Finally we arrived at a bargain. I would leave Furry there while I went on to trade in other ports. Then I would pick her up on the return voyage. He could hardly bear to let her go. That's why we are a little late."

Dick said nothing. He was too glad to have Furry with him again. But he could not help staring at the black box at the captain's feet.

"Ah, yes," the captain smiled. "I don't blame you for staring. The box is the surprise. In it you will find the king's reward for the loan of Furry."

Now it was everyone's turn to stare, for out of the box tumbled a heap of rich tapestries, jewelled swords, embroidered silks, gold coins, and precious gems.

"No, no," said Dick. "This is not for me. It should go to Mr. Fitzwarren for the shelter and protection he has given me all these years."

"Nonsense, my boy," said Mr. Fitzwarren. "This is far too great a fortune——and you owe it to your cat, not to me. But I will take care of it for you. There's more wealth in this box than I possess, plenty for you to become a merchant yourself."

The rest of the story is part of London's history. Dick (whom everyone now called Mr. Whittington) and Mr. Fitzwarren became partners. Two years later Dick married Mr. Fitzwarren's daughter, Alice, who had been in love with him for a long time. He continued to prosper until he was one of the richest men in England. As the bells had predicted, Dick Whittington became Lord Mayor of

London three times. He was knighted by King Henry the Fifth. Furry, who lived to an old age, caught mice until the very day of her death. And when she died, Dick had a figure of his beloved cat carved over his front door. The carving was so lifelike that not a single mouse ever entered the Whittington household.

FOR WANT OF A NAIL

...The Downfall of Richard the Third

For want of a nail, a shoe was lost;
For want of the shoe, a horse was lost;
For want of the horse, a rider was lost;
For want of the rider, a battle was lost;
For want of the battle, a kingdom was lost.
And all for the want of a horseshoe nail.

 HESE six lines have a general application: they show the importance of things that seem unimportant, how a trifling oversight may have tremendous results. They also have a special significance: they remind us of a particular, dramatic moment in English history.

Few men have been more hated than the fifteenth century Richard, Duke of Gloucester, who became King Richard the Third. In the opening speech in Shakespeare's historical play about him, he reveals himself as a repulsive creature, cold, cruel, and without compassion, a twisted mind in a twisted body:

I am determined to prove a villain.
And hate the idle pleasures of these days.

He stopped at nothing to further his ambitions. He had his two young nephews imprisoned in the Tower of London, and had them murdered to get rid of them because they were the rightful heirs to the throne. Then he seized the crown. However, he did not remain long in power. His treacheries were exposed; his few friends

211

turned against him and his enemies united with Henry, Earl of Richmond, to challenge his rule. It was not long before the two armies faced each other on the field of Bosworth.

Just before the battle, Richard sent a groom to see that his favorite horse was properly shod.

"You've come at a bad time," grumbled the blacksmith. "I've been busy with horses for the last two days, and I'm running short of nails. I'm not sure there's enough iron left——perhaps you'll wait while I go to the ironmonger for some more."

"No," said the groom. "I can't wait. Do the best you can—and hurry."

The blacksmith removed the old horseshoes, made new iron shoes, and fitted them to the horse's feet. Bending to complete the work, he started to hammer in the nails.

"There are enough for three of the horse's shoes," said the blacksmith, "but I'm one or two short for the left hind foot."

"Can't you make another nail?" asked the groom.

"Not unless you're willing to wait."

"I told you waiting is out of the question," said the groom impatiently. "Will the nails hold?"

"All the others will, of course. But I suppose you mean the ones on the left hind foot. Those should hold, too. I don't believe there's any real risk of a shoe coming off even with three nails—unless, of course, in an accident."

"I can't stand here arguing," said the groom. "It's a small risk, as you say, and the king will see to it that there's no accident." He hurried off.

Bosworth Field was a turmoil of men and horses. Archers were drawn up against soldiers with crossbows, pikestaffs were thrust against halberds. The fighting grew more and more disorderly; the ranks broke and the fighting became hand-to-hand. Richard rode madly among his men, urging them on with shouts and curses, heedless of all the blood that was being shed.

"Faster!" he stormed at some footmen who were not advancing rapidly enough. "Cowards!" he screamed, striking at them, urging them on with his sword. He drove his horse at them.

At that moment, the horse struck a stone. The impact loosened the shoe on his left hind foot. The horse plunged forward, fell, and threw his rider to the ground. Richard stumbled to his feet, waving his sword and calling for help.

"A horse!" he cried. "A horse! My kingdom for a horse!"

No help came. His army had dissolved. His enemies pressed closer; in another minute they were upon him. He was stabbed a dozen times.

"God and our arms be praised," said the Earl of Richmond. "The day is ours—the bloody dog is dead. Let those perish who would wound this fair land with treason. Let peace live again, and may she long live here."

"Amen," cried his followers.

The Earl of Richmond was crowned King Henry the Seventh. For want of a horse, the rider had been lost; for want of the rider, a battle had been lost; for want of a victory, a kingdom had been lost—"and all for the want of a horseshoe nail."

SIR PHILIP SIDNEY

...A Cup of Water

IR Philip Sidney was as gifted as he was handsome: he was a poet, statesman, and a soldier. He did not have to run after fame, fame ran after him. He was born noble, raised in luxury, and adored by everyone. Queen Elizabeth knighted him and appointed him governor of a province while he was still in his twenties. The queen would have liked to keep him close to her but, though he had become a great favorite, Sidney was too young and too high-spirited to remain inactive.

"Stay here," Elizabeth urged him. "You are already the favorite of the court. I will make you the jewel of my kingdom."

"Your wish is my command, your majesty," said Sidney. "But I am unfitted for a life of idleness. There is much for me to do if you will let me do it. I cannot rest contentedly in England while men are fighting—and dying—for you abroad. I pray you, give me leave to join those men."

Queen Elizabeth smiled. "I can deny you nothing," she said. "When will you go? And where?"

"Tomorrow, your Majesty," Sidney replied. "To the Low Countries where we are being so bitterly opposed."

In the Low Countries Sidney was in charge of a regiment ordered to cut off the enemy's supplies. A heavy fog made it difficult to observe troop movements, but Sidney could see enough of the road to make out a group of bulky wagons loaded with food and ammunition. He led his men to capture them. Suddenly the fog lifted and, from behind the wagons, hundreds of soldiers poured into the field.

What might have been a short skirmish grew into a pitched battle. Sidney's horse was shot from under him and, as he mounted another horse, a bullet struck him in the thigh. He fell to the ground. Two of his men made a litter and carried him to a quieter part of the battlefield.

He lay there in an agony of fever. His brow was burning, his throat parched. It was some time before a cup of cooling water was brought to him. As it was put to his lips, he saw a dying soldier staring at him.

"Give the cup to him," Sidney said. "His need is greater than mine."

It was a gallant act, and it was his last. After a few days of suffering Sidney died. His body was brought back to England and buried in Saint Paul's Cathedral with many honors.

SIR WALTER RALEIGH

...*The Courtier and the Cloak*

THE name of Sir Walter Raleigh is so well remembered because of one romantic act that we sometimes forget he was a most remarkable and many-sided man. Besides being a noble courtier, he was a poet, a soldier, a statesman, a historian, and an explorer. The great navigator, Sir Humphrey Gilbert, was his half-brother, and Raleigh was in command of the ships in 1578 when Gilbert made his first voyage to America. Later,

setting out to discover unknown lands, Raleigh founded a colony in the New World which he called Virginia, in honor of Elizabeth the Virgin Queen.

Like Sir Philip Sidney, who was two years his junior, Sir Walter Raleigh became one of the queen's favorites. We will never know whether the episode of the cloak was an actual happening or merely a cherished legend, for Raleigh was the kind of man to whom legends attach themselves. In any case, it is so truly romantic a tale that it has become part of our literature.

Queen Elizabeth, so runs the story, attended by her maids-in-waiting, was on her way to the royal barge that lay alongside the river Thames. Crowds lined the way on which she would pass. Among them was the young, splendidly dressed, scarlet-cloaked Walter Raleigh, who had recently returned to London from the wars in France and Ireland. It had rained during the night and the unpaved streets were muddy. There was a particularly large puddle in front of Raleigh, on the very spot that the queen would have to cross.

A moment later the queen herself came to the place and stopped. She looked up uncertainly, and her eyes met Raleigh's. He blushed and, without hesitation, whipped the scarlet cloak from his shoulders and spread it over the puddle. It was her turn to blush; she gave him a fleeting smile and walked on over the cloak.

It was immediately after this, according to the tale, that Queen Elizabeth conferred a title upon him, and young Walter became Sir Walter Raleigh. This much is certain: he explored with several expeditions, fought for Elizabeth on land and sea, began a new colony off the coast of North Carolina, and was the first to bring potatoes and tobacco to England. His fondness for tobacco, which he had acquired from the Indians, caused a ridiculous accident. Englishmen had never smoked before Raleigh showed them how, and it was quite a while before they got used to the sight of smoke coming out of a man's mouth. The first time that Raleigh lit a pipe in his own house, his servant was frightened.

"Help! Help!" he cried. "The master is on fire!" And, before he could be stopped, he emptied a bucket of water over Raleigh's head.

Explorer and exporter, ship-designer and inventor, adventurer and genius—Raleigh was all of these. But to millions who never heard of all these other sides of the man, he continues to be known only because of his gallant gesture with a scarlet cloak.

MARCO POLO

...*The Incredible Traveler*

HERE was never a traveler like Marco Polo. Ever since childhood he had been in love with the lure of unknown places and the sound of faraway names. He would drift into dreams whispering such words as "Cathay"... "Kermanshah"... "Kashmir" ... "Persia"... "Samarcand"... "Xanadu" ... over and over to himself.

He was seventeen in 1271 when he left Venice, his native city, with his father and uncle who were merchants. They had traveled for years in distant lands and were now about to visit the Orient. The Polos carried letters from Pope Gregory X to Kubla Khan, emperor of Cathay (as China was then called), and there they hoped to get marvelous silks, rare spices, and precious jewels.

It took three years for them to reach Cathay. But once there, they made so great an impression upon the emperor that he gave them important positions in his court, engaged them to transact business for him with strange tribes, and sent them on official missions everywhere. They remained with Kubla Khan seventeen years and before they left, Marco, who had become the special favorite of the Khan, had been made governor of one of the largest cities in Cathay. He also was the guest of honor at the palace of Chandu, which we know as Xanadu, and which was the inspiration of Coleridge's magical poem that begins:

> In Xanadu did Kubla Khan
> A stately pleasure dome decree,
> Where Alph, the sacred river, ran
> Through caverns measureless to man
> Down to a sunless sea.

In his book of travel memoirs Marco Polo describes the place this way:

> The rooms of this palace are all golden and brilliant with the most wonderful paintings of beasts and birds, with blossoms and flowering trees, all astonishing in their splendor.
>
> Around the palace is a sixteen-mile wall which encloses a forest-like park with every kind of animal, wild and tame. But even the wildest creatures have become pets. When the emperor goes hunting, leopards run along at his side.
>
> His stables are the most splendid ever seen. In them he keeps ten thousand horses, stallions and mares, all pure white without a single fleck on any of them. The males are the sturdiest in the world, and the milk of the mares is drunk by the emperor and his family because of its strength-giving power.
>
> Besides his counsellors, the emperor is greatly aided by astrologers and wizards. These can not only foretell the weather but control it; they can prevent storms and keep clouds from darkening the sky above the palace. Other magicians, experts in juggling and sleight-of-hand, can make objects appear in the air. When the emperor is seated at his table, which is on a platform eights cubits above the floor, his wine cups are set before him on another table some ten feet away. When he desires to drink, the magicians make the cups move from their places and present themselves at the emperor's right hand.

Marco Polo related many other wonders. He told of the emperor's gold and silver banquet hall that could hold six thousand guests; of his fish-charmers who never used lines and hooks but made the fish jump into their boats; of stones hung around the neck that could cure any disease; of strange sounds and sights—palm trees, pools of water, sometimes whole villages—that appear and disappear in the desert. Many of the things reported by Marco Polo seemed to be tall tales, fantasies of the imagination. But time has proved many of them to be true.

After leaving Kubla Khan's service, much to his regret, the Polos made voyages to Persia, India, Turkey, and other countries in Asia. It was twenty-six years before they returned to their home in Venice. In their padded, baggy Eastern-style pantaloons, they looked like poor vagabonds. The Venetians did not recognize them, and they were refused admission to their own house. Even when they proved who they were, the Venetians were still suspicious.

"Who could believe their outlandish stories?" said one of them. "They have turned a few odd facts into the most outrageous fantasies!"

"Marco—if he really is Marco—is the worst," said another. "He talks of such great wealth and speaks of such staggering distances that we should call him *Il Milione*, Marco Millions, instead of Marco Polo. Yet, for all his talk of Kubla Khan's generosity, I see no sign of gifts."

"He says he has planned an entertainment for next Sunday night," said a third. "It will be an odd affair if it is to be given by those shabby fellows. It is probably just a hoax. But we should go, if only to see them expose themselves."

The entertainment lived up to the promises of *Il Milione*. The guests were received in a palace that was an imitation of Kubla Khan's. There was music and dancing, and wine was served in goblets of gold. Then the banquet began. When the first course was served, Marco, his father, and his uncle appeared in robes of scarlet satin. They left the table toward the end of the dinner, and reappeared in crimson velvet trimmed with fur. The guests were astounded.

"We cannot believe what we are seeing," one of them remarked to Marco. "Is this the end of the surprises?"

"Not quite," replied Marco. "Wait and see."

The end of the banquet brought the greatest surprise of all. When the Polos disappeared, the guests expected them to come back clad in garments still more sumptuous than those they had displayed. To their astonishment their hosts reentered the hall in the shabby clothes they had been wearing when they returned from their journeys.

"What is the meaning of all this?" asked the guest who had questioned Marco. "We are amazed. Which are your real clothes— these, or the gorgeous satin and velvet robes?"

"One leads to the other," said Marco. "It is not such a mystery as it seems. Look!"

Marco ripped open the seams of the rough padded coat and took more than a hundred little packages out of the lining.

"Kubla Khan gave us many presents," he said. "But most of them were too large to carry. So we converted them into these pretty stones."

He spread upon the table a dazzling display of rubies, emeralds,

sapphires, pearls, jade, and diamonds—the greatest jewel collection the Venetians had ever seen.

"You have shamed us," said Marco's questioner. "We were wrong to doubt you. We nicknamed you *Il Milione* as a kind of joke. Now we will have to call you Marco Millions in earnest."

THE PIED PIPER OF HAMELIN

... *The Broken Bargain*

 VERYONE — or almost everyone — knows Robert Browning's poem, *The Pied Piper of Hamelin*. However, not many people know that the story itself was many hundred years old when the nineteenth century poet rewrote it. When first told it ran something like this:

Hamelin, a little German town in the duchy of Brunswick, was overrun by rats. They were so fierce and so numerous that they attacked the cats and drove the dogs out of the city. All kinds of traps were laid, but the rats just flipped them about. The creatures swarmed through the streets, broke into the houses, filled the attics, invaded the kitchens, sprang on the tables and raced through the bedrooms. They were everywhere. Browning describes them:

> Rats!
> They fought the dogs, and killed the cats,
>   And bit the babies in the cradles,
> And ate the cheeses out of the vats,
>   And licked the soup from the cook's own ladles,
> Split open the kegs of salted sprats,
> Made nests inside men's Sunday hats,
> And even spoiled the women's chats,
>   By drowning their speaking
>   With shrieking and squeaking
> In fifty different sharps and flats!

The townspeople complained bitterly. "What kind of a mayor have we got," they said, "who allows such a thing to happen! He sits in his elegant office, gazes out of the window, and does nothing about it!"

The mayor summoned his councillors, but they were no help. Day after day they met, but nothing they thought up had the slightest effect on the plague of rats. It grew worse every hour.

One summer morning—the records give the year as 1376—a tall, odd-looking stranger entered Hamelin and came straight to the town hall. Browning saw him this way:

> His queer long coat from heel to head
> Was half of yellow and half of red;
> And he himself was tall and thin,
> With sharp blue eyes, each like a pin,
> And light loose hair, yet swarthy skin,
> No tuft on cheek nor beard on chin,
> But lips where smiles went out and in—
> There was no guessing his kith and kin.
> And nobody could enough admire
> The tall man and his quaint attire.

The stranger advanced to the council table and spoke directly to the mayor.

"I hear," he said, "you are troubled with rats. I can help you, for I happen to be a rat-catcher. By means of a certain power—call it music or call it magic—I can rid your town of the pests that are such a plague to you. People call me the Pied Piper."

The mayor looked up at the man and noticed that at the end of the stranger's red and yellow scarf there hung a small pipe, and the stranger's fingers kept twitching as though they wanted to be playing on it.

"Yes," continued the strange figure, "I have freed many cities of rats, as well as gnats and bats. I will do the same for you——" he paused for a moment and coughed gently, "only you will have to pay me a thousand guilders."

"A thousand guilders?" echoed the mayor. "Make it fifty thousand! If you can really clear Hamelin of rats, it will be well worth it."

The piper stepped into the street and played a shrill tune on his pipe. As he played, rats came tumbling out of the houses. It was as if an army were on the run, murmuring and muttering. The muttering grew to a grumbling, the grumbling to a mighty rumbling, and still the rats kept coming. Great rats, small rats, lean rats, tall rats, young rats, old rats, big rats, bold rats, rats of every size and color. They followed the piper wherever he went. Still playing, he led them to the river Weser and waded in. Into the river went the rats, and there every single rat was drowned.

The piper returned to the city hall, asked politely for his thousand guilders. The mayor looked blank.

"You must be joking," said the mayor. "Surely you wouldn't expect anyone to pay such a huge sum of money for getting rid of a few rats. Besides, the river did most of the work for you. A thousand guilders? Don't be silly. Come, take fifty."

The piper's face grew dark. "I don't drive bargains," he said. "I want the full payment agreed upon. If not, you will be sorry that you didn't keep your promise. See, I still have my pipe. And if you force me, I can play a different tune."

"What!" exclaimed the mayor angrily. "You dare to threaten me! The mayor of Hamelin is not to be insulted by a fool in crazy clothes! Do your worst! Blow on your pipe until you burst!"

The piper did not say another word. Instead he left the council room and stepped out into the street. Putting his lips to the pipe, he blew again. This time the sound was anything but shrill. It was sweet and low, a dreamy tune, full of delightful turns and twists, gentle and at the same time gay, promising all manner of marvelous things. As he played, there came a sound of little hands clapping and feet pattering, of small voices chattering, like chicks in a barnyard when corn and grain are scattering. Out of the houses came boys and girls, flocking to the piper, tripping and skipping, following after the magic music with shouting and laughter.

People looked on in amazement. The mayor cried "Stop!" But the children paid no attention to anything or anyone except the piper. Singing and dancing, they followed him out of town.

This time the piper did not guide them toward the river but toward the hills. When they came to the Koppelberg, a side of the mountain opened as though it were a door and all the children— one hundred and thirty of them—trooped inside. Then the hill closed up again. Not one of these boys and girls were ever seen again.

It would never have been known what the piper's music promised, what was to be seen inside the hill, had it not been for one lame boy. He never tired of saying how dull it was in Hamelin without his playmates nor of telling what he remembered.

"Because of my lame foot," he said, "I was a little behind the others. We were all gay as on a holiday. We were all looking forward to the place the piper—I mean the piper's music—told us

about. It was a land where all things were beautiful and all people were good. A dozen rivers flowed there, each with a different sweet flavor. The flowers were larger and lovelier than anywhere else on earth. The sparrows were not dull brown as they are here, but brighter than peacocks. Dogs ran faster than deer and never barked. Bees had lost their sting. Horses were born with eagles' wings. No one was ever sad or sick, and anyone who came to the place with anything wrong—like a lame foot—was instantly cured. Just as I was about to catch up with the other children, the door in the side of the mountain closed, the music stopped, and I was left on the Koppelberg, alone."

All of this happened (or was believed to have happened) centuries ago. But still, they say, no one is allowed to play the pipe in Hamelin. Besides, they say that in Transylvania there lives a strange group who wear outlandish garments of red and yellow, and have names something like those of the families that once lived in Hamelin. Not one of them, they say, ever breaks a promise.

WILLIAM TELL

... *The Archer and the Apple*

ILLIAM TELL died in the fourteenth century, but
he continues to live not only in legend but in litera-
ture—the German poet Schiller wrote a stirring
drama about the national hero of Switzerland, and
the Italian composer Rossini glorified him in a
popular opera.

Tell was his country's greatest champion in the Swiss war of
independence against the Austrian oppressors. Albert of Austria had
determined to deprive Switzerland of its long-held freedom and
bring it under his autocratic rule. To do this he had appointed
Gessler, a real tyrant, to act as governor and subdue the people.
A group of Swiss patriots met near the Lake of Lucerne to discuss what might be done. Their leaders were three mountain-men,
Arnold von Melchtal, Walter Fürst, and William Tell.

"Gessler has sworn he will break the country into pieces," said
Arnold von Melchtal. "He has spies in every canton, and he will
punish anyone who dares to utter the word 'liberty.'"

"I have heard that he is planning something worse," said Walter
Fürst, William Tell's father-in-law. "I hear that he's going to set
his cap on top of a pole, and anyone who fails to salute it will be
thrown into jail or banished from the country."

"Our people are too proud to bend the knee to a tyrant," said
William Tell. "I, for one, would not bow to Gessler himself, let
alone his cap."

A week later Tell was walking with his seven year old son through
the town of Altdorf. There, in the center of the village square, was
a tall pole, and on top perched an Austrian cap. A dozen soldiers

loafed in front of an inn facing the village square. Tell walked by without bending his head or even glancing at the pole. The soldiers pounced upon him. Collaring the boy too, they dragged father and son to Gessler.

Gessler, dark and hateful, sat staring coldly at William Tell.

"They tell me you call yourself a patriot," he said. "They also tell me that you are quite an archer. Well, I will give you a chance to prove your skill. I could have you imprisoned, but I am a kind man. I will give you a chance."

"I do not need your 'kindness,'" said Tell.

"We shall see about that," said Gessler. "You," he said, turning to one of his soldiers, "bring me an apple. Take that boy a hundred steps from here and place the apple on his head. Now you," he said turning back to Tell, "shoot that apple off your son's head. If you do it, both of you shall go free. If you fail, both of you shall die."

The crowd that had followed from the village square gasped with horror; even the soldiers shuddered. But Tell did not flinch. He looked at Gessler with contempt. He took two arrows from his quiver, hid one inside his shirt, and silently fitted the other to his crossbow. The shaft sped to its mark—the tense silence was broken as the apple split in half and fell to the ground. The Swiss shouted for joy, while the Austrian soldiers tried not to show their admiration.

"Very pretty," said Gessler sarcastically. "But I saw you take two arrows. Evidently you weren't so sure of your first shot. You kept the second in case you should miss. Am I right?"

"You are wrong," said Tell. "The second arrow was for you had I as much as scratched my son."

"Enough!" cried Gessler. "You have spoken your own doom. Put him in chains," he told the soldiers. "Carry him across the lake to the castle at Küssnacht. Let him lie in the darkest dungeon, far from the light of the sun, and let him be a prey to the rats and reptiles that lodge there. I will go with you to see that it is done."

Tell was bound and thrown into a boat. Hardly had the vessel left the shore when the sky was covered with black clouds. A great storm sprang up bringing huge gusts of rain and driving the boat wildly in the darkness. The rowers looked helplessly at Gessler.

"If you take off my chains," said Tell, "I will guide the boat for you. I know the lake, and I am used to this kind of mountain weather."

Gessler nodded, the chains were removed, and Tell took hold of the rudder. He steered straight toward the shore, heading for a shelf of rock. Picking up his crossbow where it lay in the bottom of the boat, Tell leaped swiftly out. The rock was slippery, but Tell kept his balance. Then, as Gessler stood up in the tossing boat, he fitted the second arrow and shot the tyrant dead.

William Tell's example gave heart to other patriots. Crowds rose to challenge the rule of the Austrian oppressors. The cruel governors were killed, the land was cleared of tyranny, and the Swiss were—and have remained—a free people ever since. The rock where Tell leaped is now honored with a chapel, and a statue in the village square of Altdorf stands where the fearless archer shot the fateful apple from his son's head.

ARNOLD WINKELRIED

...*Hero of the Spears*

SEVENTY years after the triumph of William Tell, the Austrians made another attempt to take over Switzerland. The Swiss were bold and brave, but they were poorly armed. Though some had bows and arrows, and a few short swords, most of them had only crude weapons, farm utensils, scythes and pitchforks. The Austrians, on the other hand, were splendidly equipped with battle-axes, heavy shields, and long, sharp-pointed spears. The spears were particularly formidable. When the Austrian troops stood shoulder to shoulder with their long spears stretching before them, they seemed a living wall which nothing could penetrate.

The two armies met at a place called Sempach, and the Swiss archers shot their arrows with great skill. The shots glanced off the Austrians' shields and did little damage. The Swiss then charged at the enemy with everything they had, including sticks and stones, but they were easily thrown back.

"Unless we can break that line of spears," said the Swiss leader, "we are lost. If there were only some way to make a hole in that line, we might turn their army back."

"I think there is a way," said one of the soldiers. "I would like to show how it can be done."

"You seem confident," said the leader. "Who are you?"

"My name is Arnold Winkelried," replied the man. "I come from the hills of Thurgau, and I have sworn not to return until Switzerland is free of the invaders."

"What is your plan?" asked the leader.

"Watch," said Winkelried. "I will make a hole in that line!" And rushing toward the enemy, he called "Follow me! Make way for liberty!"

When he reached the Austrian line, he threw his arms wide open and gathered in a dozen or more spear-points. They pierced his body, and the Austrians could not pull their spears from his chest. Crowding around Winkelried, confused by what had happened, they milled about, no longer in an unbroken line. The Swiss hacked at them with their swords and scythes and poured through the gap made by Winkelried. Attacked from the sides and the rear, the Austrians fled. Winkelried had saved his country with his death.

There is a monument to Winkelried on the battlefield at Sempach, and his glorious deed is known throughout the world. Yet his heroism is perhaps most movingly celebrated, not in Switzerland, but by the Scottish poet, James Montgomery, in a poem that ends with the lines:

> "Make way for liberty!" he cried.
> "Make way for liberty!" and died. . .
> Thus Switzerland again was free;
> Thus death made way for liberty.

COLUMBUS AND THE EGG

...*How it Stood on End*

EVERYONE at the Spanish court—or almost everyone —laughed when Columbus said that he was going to sail over the unknown ocean to discover new lands. The Spanish nobles laughed the hardest— Columbus was not a noble, he was not even a Spaniard. He had been born in Italy and christened Cristoforo Colombo. They felt certain he could never do what he had promised.

When he returned from his first voyage to the New World they stopped laughing. They were resentful because he had proved them wrong, and they were jealous because he had been royally honored by their king and queen.

One evening a court dinner was given for Columbus as the guest of honor. The company lifted their glasses often in toasts to his exploits, and made speeches about his remarkable daring. Toward the end of the dinner one of the jealous nobles spoke.

"I do not wish to seem rude," he said. "But, after all, what is so remarkable about what you have done? A new land was discovered across the ocean. True. But the land was there. It was waiting for someone to find it—that's all. Any other man might have done it. Am I wrong?"

"You are quite right," answered Columbus. "Any other man might have done it. Just as any man can make an egg stand on its end."

"I do not understand that remark," said the noble.

"Bring me an egg," said Columbus, "and I will show you."

An egg was brought and Columbus passed it to the noble who had addressed him. "Just stand this egg on its end. It's an easy thing to do."

The noble tried, but he was not able to balance the egg so that it could stand on its end. It rolled over each time he tried.

"Would any of the other gentlemen care to make the experiment?" asked Columbus.

The egg was passed around the table. One after another failed to get it to stand upright. Finally it came back to Columbus.

"Look, gentlemen," he said, and tapped lightly against the shell. Then he placed the flattened end on the table and the egg stood up, perfectly balanced.

Everyone laughed, and the laughter was good-natured.

"Oh, come," said the noble who felt they were laughing at him. "Anyone can do that!"

"Of course," smiled Columbus. "I told you it was easy. Anyone can stand an egg on its end—or discover lands across the unknown sea. All it needs is someone first to show how to do it."

GALILEO

...The Pendulum, the Tower, and the Trial

IS name was Galileo Galilei. He was a young Italian student at the University of Pisa and, like Archimedes, he was always experimenting. He had planned to become a doctor, but a chance happening turned him into a scientist.

One late afternoon when he was about eighteen years old he was saying his prayers in the Cathedral of Pisa. A verger was lighting an oil lamp that hung from the ceiling on a long chain. Galileo noticed that the lamp swung to and fro in a regular rhythm. There seemed nothing unusual about that. Then he realized that the time it took the lamp to swing from one side to the other was exactly the same, although, as the lamp slowed down, the length of the swing was by no means the same.

Galileo rushed home to test his discovery. He took two pieces of cord of the same length and attached them to the ceiling. He fastened a piece of lead to each cord. Then he called in his godfather to count the number of motions made by one of the weighted cords, while he counted the other. One of the cords was swung in a wide arc, the other in a short one. When the two men compared the result the total was exactly the same. In spite of the difference in starting points, the two cords had taken the same time to swing and stop. Although he was not aware of it then, Galileo had hit upon the law of the pendulum, the basic law of rhythm.

The leaden weights prompted Galileo to another discovery. It had always been believed that objects of different weights fell through the air at different rates of speed. Aristotle had concluded that a ten pound weight would fall to the ground ten times faster than an object weighing only one pound. Galileo thought otherwise.

"Be careful," said his godfather. "You are just beginning your career. You will get into trouble if you dispute the scientific teachings of the great Aristotle."

"I will be careful," said Galileo. "I promise to take *great* care— to prove that Aristotle was wrong. I hope to demonstrate it at the meeting tomorrow at noon."

The place chosen for the meeting was the Leaning Tower of Pisa. All the students as well as the entire faculty of the university were there.

"He is going to make a fool of himself," said one of the old professors. "It is a pity, for he is a clever pupil. But who is he to dispute Aristotle!"

When Galileo arrived the students cheered, some of them encouragingly, some of them mockingly. The professors looked on in grim silence.

"I have two cannonballs with me," said Galileo. "One of them weighs ten pounds, the other exactly one pound. I will drop both of them from the top of this tower at the same moment. I propose to show that even a great mind can make a mistake."

Galileo climbed to the top and emerged on the gallery surrounding the top story of the tower. He rolled the cannonballs over the edge. All the students cheered when the two balls hit the ground at the same second.

Galileo had established the Law of Falling Bodies.

"I revere the teachings of Aristotle," said Galileo, "and I don't want to boast of my knowledge. But, for once, Aristotle was wrong."

Being right did not save Galileo from attack. Even his good friends felt he was going too far as he boldly attempted things that had never been done before. At twenty-eight he became an authority on military science and architecture. He invented various technical instruments such as the thermometer and a machine to draw water from the earth and irrigate the soil. He watched an optician grinding lenses in a shop and noticed how objects were magnified and brought nearer when a concave and a convex glass were held some distance from each other. The result was an improved telescope.

It was the telescope that made the most serious trouble for Galileo. With it he had discovered the satellites of Jupiter, spots on the sun, and mountains on the moon. He had seen that the bright cloud of the Milky Way was actually millions of stars. Probing the skies, he had come to the conclusion that the earth, as well as all

the planets, moved around the sun. The authorities were shocked.

"This is heresy," cried Cardinal Bellarmine. "I advise you to give up these ridiculous and irreligious ideas. Everybody knows that everything revolves about the earth because the earth is the center of the universe. For your own good, say no more on this subject."

"I will obey you," said Galileo. "I will be silent."

For a while he kept his thoughts to himself. But he could not restrain them forever. He brought out a book on astronomy which repeated his findings and made them even more positive.

"How can I do otherwise?" he asked his friends. "These are not my opinions. These are facts."

At the age of seventy, he was summoned before the Inquisition. Galileo was ill, too ill his doctor claimed to stand trial, but the heads of the Inquisition would permit no delay. "He must come at once," said the Inquisitor. "He must appear even if he has to be brought to Rome on a litter."

The trial dragged on for six months. Galileo's health grew worse as the Roman winter increased in bitterness. He was a broken man, half-dead, when he signed a paper declaring that he rejected his former heresies, that he had been wholly wrong, that his error had been one of pride and ambition, and that the earth, being the center of the universe, stands still.

"Nevertheless," he muttered, as they led him from the trial room, "it *does* move!"

THE BOY WHO STOPPED THE SEA

...A Leak in the Dike

 OLLAND is a curious country. Criss-crossed with canals, about half of it lies below sea level. The waters of the North Sea would rush over the country were it not for the dikes. The dikes are a network of walls—Hollanders learned how to make them with great mounds of earth and stone a long time ago. For centuries the dikes have saved the land from sudden storms and the daily battering of the tides. Men are constantly at work keeping the walls stout and strong, for the smallest leak must be stopped at once. Not only fields and farms, horses and cattle, but people's lives depend upon the security of the dikes.

Every boy in Holland knows this. But Willem knew it better than other boys. His father was a "sluicer," a worker at the sluice gates that guard the canals. And his uncle was in charge of a *polder*, low-lying land reclaimed from the sea and surrounded by dikes. On his way to and from school Willem used to walk along the slope of the dike as though it belonged to him. In a sense, it did, for his grandfather had directed its construction. Sometimes he would stop and pat the grassy sides of the dike with a sense of pride and possession. Sometimes he would mount to the top and stand there, looking defiantly at the sea.

One afternoon Willem was late returning from school. His class had gone on a long visit to one of the tulip gardens for which Holland is famous and daylight was fading as Willem walked along the dike on his way home. It was the beginning of a cool and quiet evening —it seemed a little too quiet. The birds had stopped singing; the wind had died down. There was no sound of anything moving except——Willem suddenly stopped! There *was* a sound, a sound he

dreaded, a sound that could bring disaster. It was the sound of water. It was not loud, only a trickle, but Willem knew what it meant. He knew that the trickle would grow; it would become a gurgle, then a little stream, then a river, a rushing torrent. And then the sea would roar over the land, sweeping away barns and houses, cattle and people, everything in a vast, angry flood.

At first Willem looked for help. But the man who inspected this part of the dike had passed a short time ago and would not be back this way for another two or three hours. Then Willem thought of going to the village where there were bags and mats that could be used to strengthen a weak place in the dike. But that would take too long, and he could see that the trickle was already beginning to widen.

There was only one thing to do, and Willem did it. He found the spot from which the water was coming—a tiny gap, a leak that could be plugged with one finger. He put his finger in the hole, and the water stopped.

For a while he felt happy, even heroic. It pleased him to think that one small boy could hold back the North Sea. Soon, too, there would be people looking for him. But, after half an hour, Willem began to worry. No one had come by, and it seemed that no one would pass for hours. It was growing dark, it was suppertime, and everyone would be at home. He called out.

"Help!" he shouted. "Help! The dike! The dike!"

But the wind and waves drowned his voice. Night had come and there was frost in the air.

Willem thought of a hundred things, of his home, of the cheerful flames in the fireplace, of his mother wondering what had happened to him, of how long it would be until someone would find him—of everything except taking his finger from the dike. He began to tremble. His teeth chattered, his finger hurt, his hand pained him, his arm began to feel cramped. His right side felt numb, his legs were weak. But he stamped his feet, and rubbed his freezing arm with his left hand to keep the blood flowing. Though he felt dizzy, he stiffened his weakening legs; he stood erect and kept his finger in the hole in the dike.

When he finally saw a man coming with a lantern, he fainted. It was his father followed by people from the village. They lifted Willem from the ground and saw the water dripping from the hole. The leak was soon effectively plugged, the dike was strengthened, and a good part of Holland was saved from a fatal flood.

And Willem became a never-forgotten legend, part of the history of Holland—the boy who had stopped the sea.

THE BELL OF ATRI

...Justice for a Horse

HE little Italian town of Atri is tucked into a hill, halfway up the Abruzzi mountains. It has a history that goes back to Roman times, but it is famous because of two things: a bell and a horse.

The bell was bronze, but it had been polished until it seemed made of burnished gold. When it was first hung in the market-place, a blast of trumpets called the townspeople together and the mayor dedicated it with a proclamation.

"This is a noble bell," he said, "but I hope it will not be heard too often. The bell is to be rung only in case of need, only if anyone has suffered unjust treatment or has been wronged in some way. I shall call it the bell of justice. Anyone, rich or poor, may ring the bell—the rope is long enough so that even a child can reach it— but no one must touch the rope unless a wrong has been done."

Many years passed. Atri was a quiet town, and its inhabitants were people of good will, honest and helpful to each other. The bell was seldom rung. It hung in the market place chiefly as a reminder that its citizens were just and honorable. Time wore away the rope and unravelled its strands. No one noticed it until the mayor spoke to his assistant about the matter.

"Age and weather have worn the rope to shreds," he said. "We must replace it."

"That isn't too easy," his assistant replied. "Strangely enough, the town doesn't have a piece of rope long enough. We must send over the mountains for a new and stronger rope."

"And in the meantime?" asked the mayor.

"Meantime I think I can provide a good substitute," said the assistant. "From the grape arbor in my garden I will cut a long grapevine and attach it to the bell. It is tough, and will surely last until the new rope arrives."

On the outskirts of Atri there lived an old knight who had once loved hunting. He had owned hawks, pure-bred hounds, and handsome horses, but of late he had become miserly. He had sold his hawks, his hounds, and all his horses except one, and that one he neglected. He spent his days counting his money and thinking of ways to increase it.

"What is the use of providing for that old horse?" he said to himself. "Now that I've stopped hunting, he is no good to me. I need him only for holidays. He's eating his head off in my stable. Let him go feed on whatever he can find."

So the poor horse was turned into the countryside to fend for himself. He wandered up and down the roads, looking for a few patches of grass or wisps of leftover hay. Farmers drove him from their fields, dogs chased him, thorny briars tore his skin. Soon he felt as miserable as he looked.

One afternoon he limped into the streets of Atri. There, in the market place, he saw a most welcome sight: a long green juicy vine. He did not hesitate, but began to nibble at the low-hanging leaves. He munched them hungrily, then pulled harder at those hanging higher on the vine. The vine did not break, and the bell began to ring.

People began to run to the market place. The mayor put on his robes and called to his assistant.

"The bell!" he cried. "The bell of justice! Someone has been wronged!"

Crowds collected. They gasped to see a horse tugging at the rope, while the bell continued to repeat with its bronze tongue:

Ding	dong
A wrong	A wrong
A wrong	has been done
Don't	be long
Repair	the wrong!

"It is the knight's neglected old horse," said the mayor. "And he is pleading his cause well. He appeals for justice, and he shall have it. Summon the knight."

"Shame!" cried the mayor, when the knight was brought before him. "That horse served you faithfully for years; it is only just that you should now serve your servant as he deserves. You have become not only a miser but an ungrateful master. There is a proverb which says 'pride goes forth on horseback grand and gay, but comes back on foot and begs the way.' Curb your pride, and share your wealth. I remind you of the law of justice. This steed served you in youth, so you shall comfort him in his old age. Shelter him in a decent stall and see that he is properly fed."

The knight hung his head. He led the old horse back home while the crowd cheered. The mayor smiled.

"Church bells," he said, "ring us to come to church, but they cannot make us go in. My bell does more: it comes right into court and pleads the cause of creatures who cannot speak for themselves."

In *Tales of a Wayside Inn* Longfellow ends his poems about the bell and the horse with these lines:

> And this shall make, in every Christian clime,
> The bell of Atri famous for all time.

THE MOUSE-TOWER ON THE RHINE

...A Perfect Punishment

 N the first place it wasn't a mouse-tower but a watchtower. It had been built in Bingen in the Middle Ages by Hatto, who used it as a lookout and also as a toll house for collecting duties on all goods that passed up and down the Rhine. In the second place, it would have made the town of Bingen proud if Hatto had not been so miserly, so calculating and so cruel.

There was no question about Hatto's greediness. He was rich enough, but he dreamed of being richer. He thought only about money and ways of making more. He was jealous of anyone who had a few pennies or enjoyed a few pleasures. He owned several farms but he grudged the poor farmers their food. He grudged the mice the few crumbs they could find in his larder and he grudged his cats their few mice.

The richer he got the more unsatisfied he was with what he had. He kept on raising taxes—no boat, not even the smallest barge, could pass his tower without paying a toll out of all proportion to what it carried. Hatto's thin hands were as cold as the silver coins he loved to caress. His fingers grew longer and leaner while his money bags grew fatter and firmer.

Everyone suffered one autumn when the crops failed and the country was faced with famine—everyone except Hatto. Hatto had prepared for just such an emergency. He had stocked his barns and silos with grain and other fodder; even the attics were crammed with corn. What the farmers needed badly, he sold at an enormous profit; when they came for more, he raised the prices. At last the money stopped rolling in. The farmers were bankrupt. Their families were starving and there was no work for them to do.

They appealed to Hatto. They came to him by twos and threes, then by dozens, then by hundreds. He had the same answer for all.

"Buy at the market while you can. Tomorrow the prices will be higher."

Hatto shut himself up in his mansion, but he could not avoid the starving people. Big-eyed children begged at his door; haggard women held their infants up to his windows. Finally Hatto seemed to relent. He came out to talk to them.

"I sympathize with you," he said. "I understand the situation, and I have decided to do something about it. Tomorrow morning all those who need help should assemble in my old barn—the large empty one on the hill—and I promise there will be an end to your suffering."

The crowd went home rejoicing.

Next morning all the village families, gaunt-cheeked and hollow-eyed, gathered in the barn and waited for the corn and grain they hoped would be distributed. They did not have to wait long.

When the last man, woman, and child were packed in the building, Hatto bolted the doors. For a moment the poor people were too stunned to realize what was happening. They could not believe that anyone would play such a cruel joke on them. Then, when they saw it was not a joke, they pounded on the doors, cried, and screamed to be let out. The doors remained closed, and the trapped victims were too weak to break them down. There was no help for the people. Gradually they starved to death, vainly weeping for mercy.

"Listen to the field mice twitter!" said Hatto as their cries grew fainter. "Lazy vermin, all of them. Now, at last, there'll be an end to their begging and whining. May I be bitten by a mouse if I'm mistaken."

For several months the dead were undisturbed; the bones lay unburied. Then all at once, the bones disappeared and the place was clean. No one knew how or where the bones had gone. Hatto shrugged his shoulders.

"Dust to dust," he said. "Good riddance to rubbish. And that includes mice as well as men."

Then one day, while Hatto was counting his money in his deepest vault, he noticed a mouse where no mouse had ever penetrated. The mouse sat staring at him with a most unmouselike expression. Hatto shouted at the creature. The mouse did not move. Hatto threw something at the animal, and the creature disappeared.

After that Hatto found mice wherever he went. He looked to his cats for help, but there was no longer a cat in sight. The kitchen

swarmed with mice, the bedrooms were overrun, the halls, the pantry, and all the closets were crowded with them. They were afraid of nothing. They sprang on his table and snatched his food; they frisked their tails in his wine; they tore up blankets and counterpanes and made nests in his beds. Increasing by thousands every day, they devoured everything in his larder. When nothing was left, they began on his warehouses, on his barns and silos. Hatto's corn vanished, so did his grain. When the last bit had been eaten, they chewed up his wood. He could hear them scurrying in his walls, getting ready to gnaw through the wainscoting.

Fearing that the whole house would tumble down, Hatto fled to his watchtower on the Rhine. There he began to breathe easier. The tower had stone walls; it was on an island. Between it and the shore was the river and there was always a strong current—much too strong for anyone to swim, especially mice . . . and Hatto doubted that mice could swim.

He spent the first day in the tower checking up on the provisions he had stored there for emergencies. On the second day, he began to count the money he had stored away. On the third day Hatto happened to look out of a high window and could not believe what he saw. He saw the blue Rhine turn black. When he looked closer he realized it was black because the river was full of dark-furred creatures—mice, millions and millions of mice. They were—there was no doubt about it—swimming, swimming steadily, paddling with their paws, steering with their tails, swimming slowly but surely toward the tower. Hatto thought he could hear them squeaking to each other—"twittering like field mice," he thought.

Hatto ran about in panic. He mounted to the highest room in the tower, locked himself in, and put heavy bags—money bags—against the doors. Then, breathing heavily, he waited.

He did not have to wait long. He heard the whisper of a million little feet pattering up the stairs, then the sound of more millions gnawing through wood. Then, in a last desperate effort to distract the invaders, Hatto opened the door and threw bread, corn, and even meat to the army of mice. But they were not hungry for what he offered. They had come for a different kind of food.

Some weeks later, when workmen were sent to the tower, they found Hatto's provisions undisturbed. But they did not find Hatto. All they found were some fragments that looked like bones scattered among his money bags.

TILL EULENSPIEGEL

...His Merry Pranks

 HIS is the story of a rogue, a rascal, a scamp, a scapegrace, a knave, a ne'er-do-well, a deceiver, a cheat, a trickster——there aren't enough words to describe what a scoundrel he was. He thought life was a joke, a joke that was on somebody else. Even his name was a joke: Till Eulenspiegel, a German name suggesting an owl looking at himself in a mirror. The English called him Owlglass. He played tricks on everyone—innkeepers and nobles, princes, as well as peasants—and, though he was often in trouble, he was always quick to get out of it. He even escaped the gallows because of his wit.

He started fooling people when he was a boy. His father, a poor Brunswick farmer, had died and his mother was unable to provide for her son and herself. Till was an idle lad, too fond of fun to do any of the chores around the farm.

"You're never here when I need you," his mother complained. "When the cow should be driven in for the night, or firewood gathered, you are nowhere in sight. If you don't like life on a farm, you should find work elsewhere."

"Oh," said Till, airily, "work is all right for those who like it. I have other plans. Don't worry about me. I can take care of myself."

"And who is going to take care of the farm, or me?" said his widowed mother bitterly. "Your so-called plans will not feed us. We don't have enough food to last another day. There isn't even a piece of bread in the house."

"Why didn't you say so?" asked Till, innocently. "If it's bread you want, you shall have it—all you want of it."

"And how are you going to get it?" asked his mother. "Are you going to buy it without money and bake it without flour?"

"You shall see," said Till and left the house whistling. He walked briskly into a town where he was not known and swaggered boldly into the best bakery.

"I bring you an order from Duke Wilhelm," he said. "The duke has received an unexpected company of nobles and, for tomorrow's breakfast, he needs a large quantity of your finest breads."

"How many loaves will the duke require?" asked the baker. "And what kind does he prefer?"

"Thirty should do. The duke wants an assortment—of your very best, mind you," said Till. "Some white, some dark, some rye. And while you're about it," he added lightly, "you might put in a dozen or so of those sweet buns and poppy seed rolls. Yes, that ought to be enough."

The baker was happy to have the order, but he was a little suspicious. This lad, he thought, might be one of the duke's new servants; on the other hand, he might be an impostor.

"I will send the bread and rolls to the duke's palace a little later," said the baker. "Besides, it would be too large a bundle for you to carry alone."

"The duke wants the order at once," said Till. "But if you're afraid to trust me, send your boy along. We will share the load, and he will see that it is delivered to the duke's kitchen."

This satisfied the baker, and Till and the baker's boy started off toward the duke's palace. They had not gone far when Till managed to drop a couple of loaves in the gutter.

"Oh dear!" he said to the boy. "This will never do. The duke's cook would throw the whole lot back at us if she saw the smallest speck of dirt on a loaf. Take these back to the baker and get two clean ones. I'll wait here until you return."

As soon as the baker's boy was out of sight, Till went off in another direction to his home.

"Look!" he said to his mother. "Here's bread enough for months! Whatever you can't eat, you can sell. Whatever you can't sell, you can make into puddings and stuffing. You see, we need never go hungry."

When Till was about nineteen there was a fair held in a neighboring county. Till stole a horse. Then, clapping his heels against the animal's sides, he rode clattering through the fair grounds, scattering pots and pans, breaking crockery and making the ground shake with the horse's thundering hooves. When the tradesmen threatened to thrash him, Till said: "Good people, you must pardon me. I'm a little excited because I just saw a most amazing thing. I saw a cow with her head where her tail should have been, and her tail where her head ought to be."

When they jeered at him, Till said: "I see you don't believe me. You think I am joking. Well, I can assure you it's true. If each of you will give me a five-penny piece I'll prove that I'm right. Come and see. And if I haven't told you the truth, I'll not only give you back your coins but I'll pay for any damage I may have done."

Everyone was so eager to see the unbelievable freak that Till had no trouble collecting a great many coins. Then he led them to a barn at the edge of the fair grounds. There they saw an ordinary cow, but they had to confess that Till had told them the truth. It was tied the wrong way—perhaps Till himself had tied it—with its tail tied to the feedbox and its head sticking out of the door.

Some laughed, some shook their fists at Till. He held up his hands and said, "Just a moment. Don't be angry with me. A joke is a joke, and you must take it with a laugh. At the same time, I'll give one of you a chance to get his money back. I'll do better than that. I'll give my own good horse to the man who lets me give him three good sharp blows between his shoulder blades."

The men looked at each other. A whack on the back is not a pleasant thing. But three thumps, even hard ones, are a small price to pay for a fine horse.

"Here!" cried one of the fellows. "I'm your man. Go ahead."

Till delivered a tremendous blow just below the man's neck.

"Ow!" cried the victim. "That hurt! But let's have the other two."

Again Till smote the man, and again the poor fellow cried out. "That was a terrible blow—I can't stand much more of this. Now let's have the third stroke, and I'm glad it will be the last."

"I'm not ready for the third one," said Till, grinning. "I said you could have the horse after three blows, and you'll have to wait for the third. I'm in no hurry—some other day will do."

All the others, glad that they were not the ones tricked, laughed as Till shrugged his shoulders and slipped away. This time he journeyed quite a distance. He was scarcely twenty years old when he reached Regensburg and went to the chief hospital.

"I am a traveling doctor," he told the manager of the hospital, "and I have my own methods for dealing with sick people. No drugs, no potions, no powders. But I guarantee that I can cure every patient in this building."

"That's a large claim," said the superintendent. "How long will your treatment take? And how much money will you expect if you accomplish these remarkable cures?"

"My method always succeeds," said Till. "It never takes more than a single day. As for payment, my fee is three hundred florins, and I will want one hundred in advance. If my method fails, you need not pay me as much as a penny more, and I will return the hundred florins."

"Fair enough," said the manager. "When will you start?"

"Tomorrow morning," said Till.

Early the next day Till entered the hospital. He went from bed to bed, whispering the same thing to all the patients. "Listen carefully," he said. "One of you must be sacrificed for the others. One patient—the sickest one—must be put in an oven and cremated. From his ashes I will prepare a medicine for the rest of you. First, however, I will call the superintendent and we will find out who among you is the sickest and, therefore, the one to be sacrificed."

When the superintendent came, Till cried out: "All those who feel they are now able to leave their beds, get up at once and go. Anyone who is too sick, remain in bed."

The trick worked. No one wanted to be sacrificed. Every patient managed to get out of the hospital. Till jingled the coins in his pocket and left Regensburg in a hurry. He did not wait to find out what would happen when the patients returned.

At twenty-one Till was employed as court jester to Count Karl of Magdeburg. The count enjoyed Till's wit, but he prided himself that Till could never get the better of him.

"Your highness is quite right," said Till one evening when the count had told a story that he claimed was funnier than any of Till's. "I know your mind is the best in all Germany. I even know things about you that nobody else knows."

"Is that so?" said the count. "For example?"

"Well," said Till. "I know that you have a strawberry-shaped mark under your left shoulder blade."

"You know what doesn't exist," laughed the count. "There isn't a mark of any kind on my body."

"I will bet fifty florins that I am right," said Till, stubbornly.

"It will be a shame to take your money," said the count. "But since you are so positive I accept the bet."

The count took off his clothes and proved there was no mark below his left shoulder blade or anywhere else.

"I have made a fool of myself," said Till. "As usual, you are perfectly right. Here is the money."

That night as his manservant was helping him undress, the count said, "What nonsense have you been telling Till about there being a strawberry-shaped mark below my left shoulder blade."

"Your Highness," stammered the servant. "It would never occur to me to discuss anything relating to you with anyone. I never said a word about you to Till."

"That's curious," said the count. "I wonder what prompted him to make so foolish a bet. He certainly looked silly when I undressed and proved how wrong he was."

"Oh, oh! I see it now!" exclaimed the servant. "The wretch! The scoundrel! This morning he boasted that he could do anything he set his mind to, that he could even make you take off your clothes! I bet him a hundred florins—my entire savings—that he could not do it. He did it, the impudent villain! He lost fifty florins to you, but won a hundred florins from me. He's fifty florins ahead!"

"Till is a clever practical joker," admitted the count. "But he will have to practice his jokes elsewhere. His days as a court jester are over."

The count was right. Till wandered from place to place, from one odd job to another. But he never stopped playing tricks. He found a dead rabbit, skinned it, and put a kitten inside it. Then he sold it to a collector of rare animals as the only rabbit ever born that could purr, mew, and run after mice. Annoyed with Till's pranks, Heinrich, Baron of Bemberg, ordered Till off his land. Whereupon Till bought a cartload of earth for a few pennies and, seating himself on top of it, drove through Bemberg. When the baron threatened to put Till in prison for being on his private property, Till said, "I am not on your land; I am on my own. I bought this earth from a farmer and, since it is my land, I have a right to ride around on it."

He managed to get a common donkey and show it at county fairs. He charged a penny admission to see and hear "The Only Educated Donkey in the World." When the donkey brayed "Ee-ah, Ee-ah," Till told the spectators, "See how fast he learns! Last week he couldn't read a word, and now he is learning the alphabet. He already knows the two principal letters—"E" and "A"—and how beautifully he pronounces them!"

Once, when Till was found robbing a store in Bremen, he was brought into court. "You have done your last wicked deed," said the judge. "For this and your many other crimes, I condemn you to be hanged. Take him to the gallows."

When the noose was put around his neck, Till said, "It's a pity to waste such a fine new rope on such a worthless fellow as me. I suggest that you let me go home—I have some old rope there and I will hang myself. That way you'll be saving the hangman's fee as well as the cost of a new rope."

This seemed reasonable enough, so they let Till go. As he ran away from the gallows, he called back, "Don't worry that I won't keep my word. I will certainly go home, and I will hang myself— if I can ever spare the time."

Till remained a fun-maker until the day of his death. When they came to bury him, the neighbors found a piece of paper on his bed. It was in Till's handwriting and it read:

"This is the Last Will and Testament of Till Eulenspiegel. Although I have neither money nor land to bequeath, I leave something which is equally valuable. To you, my friends, I leave a chest

of precious stones. I leave it on one condition: it is not to be opened until after my burial."

The funeral was a hasty one. The neighbors hurried through the ceremony. They could not wait to get back to the huge chest that was standing in a corner of Till's shabby room. When it was opened, they found another piece of paper under the lid. This one read:

"Rich men may have rubies and diamonds and other such jewels. The stones I leave are far more precious. They are building stones, stones for houses to keep you warm, and stones for churches to keep you good. Thus you will be good *and* warm. Therefore they are truly precious stones. Use them carefully."

In death, as in his life, Till had the last laugh.